THE FUTURE
OF OUR PAST

THE FUTURE OF OUR PAST

The Spanish Mystics
Speak to
Contemporary
Spirituality

SEGUNDO GALILEA

AVE MARIA PRESS
Notre Dame, Indiana

Library of Congress Catalog Card Number: 85-71822

International Standard Book Number: 0-87793-295-6 (Cloth)

0-87793-296-4 (Paper)

Cover design by Elizabeth J. French

Printed and bound in the United States of America

CONTENTS

FOREWORD

Lately, in lectures and retreats in both South and North America I've been stressing the importance of the best Christian mystical tradition with regard to our current spiritual challenges.

As a Spanish American, I'm particularly interested in the great Spanish mystics, Teresa of Avila, John of the Cross, and Ignatius Loyola. As a Catholic priest, concerned with the mission of the church in today's world, I'm equally concerned about how to bring a strong spirituality into the liberation theology thinking and its ensuing commitments.

This book is the result of these concerns, proposed in several lectures and discussions, in Spanish or in English, on how the mystics can enlighten and inspire some of our current Christian endeavors. Therefore, this work is not intended to be an overall research on the Spanish mystics' doctrines, nor a synthesis of their spirituality. It is, rather, a collection of meditations in the manner of spiritual reading, covering some areas of Christian life in which I find the Iberian mysticism specially relevant.

—Segundo Galilea

A
Spirituality
for Today

A Spirituality for Today

It is a truism that today, in all sectors of the church, there is a growing interest in the subject of spirituality. This was not always the case. For a long time, in fact, spirituality was something taken for granted. It was always there in the background, of course, but by the same token it aroused little special attention. For example, when I was receiving my Christian formation, everyone accepted the importance of prayer, frequent communion and confession, the need for spiritual reading and counseling, and the value of asceticism and certain devotions. One did these things as best one could, with the understanding that such spiritual practices were essential for anyone who wanted to be a good Christian.

During the past two decades, a number of theological and pastoral issues have come to the fore, especially in matters affecting the relationship between Christian life and the real world we live in. Although we cannot analyze or evaluate them here, we can say that these issues, sometimes involving personal and community crises, also led to a lack of interest in some of the core questions of spirituality. This can be seen, among other things, in the absence of such questions from theological and pastoral literature, and from the agendas of study groups organized both here and in Europe, whether on the level of the hierarchy or on any other level. Interest tended to focus on other areas that seemed, understandably, more urgent to the church at the time. The fact is, however, that spirituality and faith-experience, which should have been the very backbone of these other areas of concern, were not sufficiently stressed.

It seems obvious that this attitude has changed during the last few years, and although we are probably not entitled to say that there is more spirituality in the church today than before, we can safely state that explicit interest in spirituality is much greater now. Topics of spirituality appear frequently in books, monographs, magazine articles and study groups. Nowadays, too, there is a manifest desire among people to express and celebrate their faith-life in communities and in various church movements.

It is interesting to note that these indications cut across all currents of thought and pastoral practice. They appear among both "progressive" and "traditional" groups, in both "popular" and "elitist" approaches, both within liberation theology and outside it—to mention but a few of the more common labels presently in vogue. We have even seen the rise of whole new movements devoted to spirituality (the charismatic renewal, for one), as well as a serious search within movements mainly concerned with human rights and the liberation of the oppressed for a Christian mystique to support their quest.

Certainly, this whole matter needs to be more carefully evaluated since not everything in it has the same Christian and pastoral influence or importance for the church's mission. Often enough, these different spiritual trends and expressions seem to have little mutual understanding and hence, rightly or wrongly, they tend to question other groups, either as to the degree of their incarnation in contemporary reality, or to the Christian character of that incarnation. Some of them stress a spirituality in action, while others stress a spirituality of evangelical identity in contrast to a world that is strongly resistant to change.

Likewise, it seems premature to speak of a spiritual renewal in the church. Doubtless this will come, and it will be needed in order to deepen and consolidate all the good things that have been emerging in Christianity during the last decades. The present trend is more of an awakening, and the evangelical quality of the language it uses — reflecting its preferential option for the poor and its experience of God as leading to solidarity and peace — should not blind us to the fact that Christian practice, which is the vital point in mysticism, does not always respond to ideals. It is one thing to be sincerely convinced of something and another to live up to those convictions.

But we are basically concerned here with two things: the fact that there is an interest in and an explicit search for spirituality, and the fact that this search can be a significant and valid adjunct to the mission of Christianity.

The idea of a spirituality for our times needs some clarification. This does not mean a spirituality that is original, new, or based only on current Christian experience. We are well aware that any authentic mysticism is in continuity with the universal Christian tradition.

To speak of a spirituality for our times is to speak of certain cultural values typical of North and South American Christianity; it is to speak of certain missionary challenges, and certain significant and current Christian experiences. These new spiritual trends are, in turn, demands and components that both tinge and stimulate the diverse spiritualities that live together in the church. Ignatian, familiar, monastic and lay spiritualities must, without losing their identity, become permeated with this "new" Christian experience, because they are rooted in and express themselves within the churches of North and South America. This, without doubt, will help them to live their distinctive emphases and charisms in a better and fuller way.

One good example of this is the Latin American experience of the religious life. This is composed of many congregations and spiritualities. Nevertheless, the fact that they are rooted and carry out their mission in a culture which has similar Christian challenges allows them to live with an emphasis on certain common values such as those formulated at Puebla for Latin America: the experience of God united to mission, community lived as fraternity, a preferential option for the poor and the abandoned, a sense of mission from and within the local church. These emphases tend to become components of what could be called a spirituality of religious life in Latin America, in which various congregations and schools of spirituality share, since it is for all of them a renewing experience.

Speaking along general lines, we may say that contemporary spirituality shows a preference for certain themes and experiences:

-the experience of God in our history and in our mission; rediscovering, in this context, the value of contemplation and prayer;
-knowing, loving and following the historical Jesus

through the power of the Spirit as the criterion and
way in our life of Christian practice;
-the primacy of effective fraternal love in spirituality;
solidarity, communion and sharing, reconciliation,
the practice of justice and mercy, work for peace
and for a new international order;
-a preferential option for the poor and for their integral liberation as a privileged way of following
Jesus and leading a life of effective love; evangelical
poverty as a condition of this love, and as a criticism
of the affluent and consumerist society; solidarity
with poor and dependent countries;
-the contribution of the spiritual experience of the
laity, and in particular that of women.

The Spanish Mystics

The spiritual search we have envisioned would like to avoid
what many have rightly or wrongly termed the deformations
of traditional piety. These deformations would generally in-
clude certain practices and attitudes which, although they accompanied an effective search for holiness, were nevertheless
conditioned by a particular cultural background and by a concept of the human person and of secular realities which most
of us today would consider inadequate and even harmful.
The same could be said of certain theological commonplaces
that were dominant in the spiritualities of the past.

The fact, which is not always easy to discern or interpret,
has had the unfortunate effect of distancing our generation
from the classics of spirituality, since their cultural and
linguistic categories do not jibe with ours. But unless we take
the trouble to reinterpret the cultural and religious language
of the great spiritual masters, we will be depriving ourselves
of access to the wealth of their experience and their message.
Thus we impoverish ourselves and are cut off from the best
spiritual tradition of Christianity. Indeed, unless we recover

that great tradition and incarnate it in our own context, no real revival of mysticism can take place.

Three Great Reformers

All renewal, all creativity in Christian experience, should be nourished on the best spiritual tradition in the church. Only thus will it be possible to incarnate the gospel in the realities and challenges of history. Tradition and incarnation are constant reference points in every spirituality. The more we search for a spirituality for today, the more we must identify with the heart of the church, with her best tradition, and with the most valid roots of her spirituality. And, speaking of this tradition and these roots, we cannot afford to ignore the exceptional and decisive role played by the 16th-century Spanish mystics in the history of spirituality. Their influence is still alive and valid for today.

The best tradition in the Iberian spirituality of the 16th century is condensed in the experience and teachings of three great Spanish saints: Ignatius of Loyola, Teresa of Avila and John of the Cross. This is not to say that they have been influential in all cases, or even in an explicitly acknowledged way, either in the period of the emergence of Christianity in the New World, or even later. Their relevance in modern spirituality is of a more sweeping and radical character: These great mystics have left a decisive mark on all spirituality from the 16th century onward, from Rose of Lima to Thomas Merton.

The strongest and most solid devotions and attitudes in popular religious expression, particularly in Latin America, are historically Iberian in origin and, in many instances, are identical with the themes and Christian experiences of these three mystics. The same is true of the spirituality of the Catholic elite in all of the Americas. No one can deny the very early Ignatian and Teresian influences on the clergy and on religious life and, through them, on the devotion and spirituality of the people.

The Historical Synthesis

We have already alluded in passing to Ignatian spirituality, which was influential not only in the apostolic field of the Jesuits but also among the secular clergy and important sectors of the most cultured laity. The same is true of the spirituality of both Carmelite reformers, whose influence has always been operative especially among congregations of women.

There are, of course, other trends of spirituality that have had a more or less explicit influence on the New World. Among them we should mention the trend begun by St. Francis de Sales whose works, *An Introduction to the Devout Life* and *Treatise on the Love of God* (17th century), were widely read by past generations. Yet even here it should be remarked that the humanism which characterizes them shows Ignatian influences, while his doctrine on prayer and love has its roots in Teresa. Indeed, her influence on these works is obvious. These influences are to be found in all modern schools of spirituality in France (the "French School").

In this connection, another outstanding case is the spirituality of St. Térèse of Lisieux whose writings enjoyed a wide circulation in the Americas during the first half of the 20th century and are now enjoying a kind of critical rediscovery. The doctrine of the French saint is obviously the outcome of her own creativity and experience, though we must never forget that she was a spiritual daughter of Teresa of Avila. More recently, the spirituality stemming from the witness and writings of Charles de Foucauld has had an extensive influence on, among others, the Spanish-speaking world. This spirituality is considered one of the best expressions of the French tradition, as well as one of the peaks of the spirituality of this century, which otherwise seems to have produced only a few masters of spirituality. De Foucauld is an avowed disciple of St. Teresa and St. John of the Cross. Their writings were his favorites, after the Bible.

If the above-mentioned Spanish mystics have become an almost obligatory reference for the development of Christian spirituality from the 16th century onward, this is due to the fact that, taken together, they constitute the best synthesis of the spiritual tradition of the preceding centuries. Aside from this, 16th-century Iberian mysticism is also the historical watershed marking the confluence of medieval mysticism and the contemplative tradition of the Christian East. We now turn to an examination of this fact, at least in very broad outline.

The Eastern Tradition in Iberian Spirituality

The great synthesis forged by the Spanish mystics includes, in some way, the contemplative tradition of the Christian East, the roots of which go back to the Desert Fathers.

The best representative of this synthesis is St. John of the Cross. To start with, it should be borne in mind that Carmel, as a school of spirituality, was born in Palestine where it was engrafted into the tradition of Eastern monasticism. When the Carmelites later migrated to England and other parts of Europe, they integrated this spiritual experience into their spiritual synthesis.

The doctrine of God-filled silence, detachment and prayer which we find in Teresa and John, and which has become classic in Christian monasticism, had its cradle in the deserts of Palestine, Syria and Egypt. St. John of the Cross, like other mystical theologians who were his contemporaries, was influenced by the writings of pseudo-Dionysius, an important witness to this tradition and one of the few authors (aside from the Bible) cited by the mystical Doctor. His influence on St. John's conception of union with God, and even on his terminology, is noteworthy.

But there is yet another aspect in which Eastern spirituality shows some affinity with Iberian spirituality — and perhaps even more so with popular devotion — namely, in its method of prayer. This prayer method, hesychasm, is exemplified in the Jesus Prayer and had its origins in the Desert Fathers who emphasized the kind of prayer that passes through the "heart." The hermit's Prayer of the Heart is a sort of litany, an ever-repeated scriptural prayer: Lord Jesus Christ, Son of God, have mercy on me, a sinner! If this prayer is repeated on the lips while the mind is fixed on Jesus, its repetition moves gradually into the affections, transforming it into a Prayer of the Heart, so that it becomes more and more contemplative with each successive utterance.

I think that the Christian West has adapted this form of prayer in the patterns of its various litanies. I also see vestiges of this prayer-form in the recitation of the rosary with its persistent repetition of Hail Marys after an initial fixing of the mind on some mystery in the life of Christ or Mary.

I know of so many Christians who have given up saying the rosary and litanies simply because they found them too routine and elementary, prayers for beginners only. I had the same experience until I discovered that, far from being prayers for beginners, the rosary and litanies are forms of mystical prayer, and that the constant repetition of a brief, heartfelt formula could bring one to a true and expressive contemplation. The greater the contemplative quality of one's prayer, the greater the benefit one derives from the rosary and litanies. The same principle is at work here as that which inspired the Jesus Prayer of hesychasm, as well as the most traditional forms of contemplative prayer in Christian spirituality.

Further, people have a great liking for this form of prayer.

The rosary, litanies, vocal prayer and the refrains of well-known hymns are popular devotions. We know that in repetitive prayer, as in almost any devotion, ambiguous or decadent attitudes can creep in, depending on the quality of the pastoral or pedagogical content that accompanies them. But the very popularity of these forms of prayer should remind us of the contemplative potential among the faithful, and that this potential could be led, through these simple means, toward a true Prayer of the Heart.

The foresight of the first missionaries in the Americas in introducing the best European songs and litany-like prayers, especially the rosary, was a stroke of genius. Today we speak of utilizing popular religiousness in evangelization, and here we have a devotional trait which not only corresponds to the contemplative vocation of the Christian people, but has roots sunk deep in one of the richest experiences in Christian mysticism, a synthesis between devotion and liturgy, emotion and doctrine, the popular and the elite. Such a synthesis is necessary for balance in Christian spirituality. It existed in the Iberian peninsula and in the Americas in the 16th and 17th centuries, although it later went into a decline. Here, too, the experience of the mystics, with their great appreciation for the affective dimension of prayer, is very much to the point.

The Northern Mystics and the Devotio Moderna

The mystical tradition of the West, to which 16th-century Spanish spirituality belongs, achieved a clear, high-level synthesis in Carmelite and Ignatian mysticism.

St. John of the Cross, the most cultured and learned of the 16th-century mystics, had read the authors who had been most influential on Western spirituality in the preceding centuries and incorporated the best of their thought in his writings. The Carmelite saint not only was acquainted with the best exponents of the Rheno-Flemish mysticism of the Late Middle Ages (Ruysbroeck, Meister Eckhart and, above all, Tauler), but also utilized the contributions of the English mystics who achieved great prominence in the 14th century and with whom the Carmelites were familiar. (It should be remembered that Carmel had its European beginnings in England.) In John of the Cross' doctrine we can perceive some affinity with that of the unknown author of *The Cloud of Unknowing* who was perhaps the best exponent of Medieval English mysticism. It might be remarked in passing that St. Teresa manifests an analogous affinity with the mysticism of Julian of Norwich.

In the light of his own mystical experience and theological background, St. John of the Cross restored what was best in these schools, forging them together in an original synthesis which avoided certain of their limitations, such as the excessive intellectualism of the Rhinelanders. St. Ignatius and St. Teresa were to do something similar with respect to the *Devotio Moderna*.

The *Devotio Moderna*, nourished on the mystical tradition of the High Middle Ages, was in part a reaction—one that was widely and gladly welcomed—to the excesses of Scholastic rationalism in spirituality. It was also a response to the more or less constant divorce between academic theology and practical spirituality. The *Devotio Moderna* was affective, stressing intimacy with Jesus and setting a higher value on Christian practice than on discursive knowledge. Its best-known exponent was Thomas à Kempis, whose *Imitation of Christ* is surely the most-read book of spirituality, aside from the Bible, in church history.

The influence of the values of the *Devotio Moderna* is palpable in the works of St. Ignatius, and even more so in those of St. Teresa. It is a matter of record that St. Ignatius, during his retreat at Manresa, read and re-read the *Imitation of Christ.* Its influence on the *Spiritual Exercises* is undeniable, and is borne out by his distinctive Christocentrism and the importance he attaches to affective prayer. We will return to this theme later.

"Affective Christocentrism" is also characteristic of St. Teresa, who doubtless read some of the books of the "modern devotion" in the early years of her religious life and was greatly influenced in later life by her Jesuit confessors. When she writes that prayer "is not a matter of thinking much, but of loving much" (*Interior Castle*, Fourth Mansions, Ch. 1, par. 8). She is acting as a channel for some of the riches of the "modern devotion." In this, too, she is a representative of the spirituality of her people, to whose devotions she always felt a certain nearness.

It is not enough for us, however, to affirm the convergence of the church's spiritual tradition in the work of the Spanish mystics. We still have to ask what significance this synthesis has for Christian experience and the search for a spirituality for today. In short, do the Spanish mystics have anything significant to tell us here and now?

The Relevance of the Great Mystics

Since so few people, aside from specialists, read these mystics today, what can they possibly have to tell us? Can they say anything at all to contemporary Christians seeking ways to profess their faith amid a world of overwhelming challenges? What relevance can they have for people involved in the peace movement, in the struggle for justice and human rights, in the search for reconciliation beyond the barriers of discrimination and racism? What message do they have to offer to a church eager to renew itself so as better to fulfill its evangelizing mission—today and tomorrow—in a secularized, materialistic and permissive society? What light or inspiration can they offer Christians who feel called to follow

Jesus along a path strewn with conflict, idolatry and lies, a path on which the witness of persecution and loneliness is not just a hypothetical possibility?

Let us begin to answer these questions by pointing out that the mystics we have mentioned are part of the heritage of the whole church. The fact that they belonged to a particular order or congregation is quite secondary in view of their message for all humanity. Before he was ever a Jesuit, Ignatius was a man of the church, and his spiritual message far transcends the limits of a particular religious community or school of spirituality. The same can be said of the Carmelite mystics. All of them belong to the classics of Christian spirituality. Theirs is a message for all seasons, for Christianity as a whole.

It is first and foremost as witnesses of the church and as classic representatives of the Ibero-American Christian tradition that these mystics can help us to become integrated into the mainstream of the Holy Spirit's action in America and to get in touch with the roots of our spiritual wealth and identity.

As we shall see later, they can help us to confirm and reinforce our own spiritual search within their great tradition by providing themes, insights and experiences on which to nourish it. They can likewise correct and give greater depth and solidity to our searching, by placing it in a broader, and at times more authentic, perspective. In 1982, as we recalled the fourth centennial of St. Teresa's death, we were not just recalling a past that might have been able to inspire us in another context. Rather, we were recalling the roots of our present and a tradition which, whether we realize it or not, forms part of our present Christian identity.

These reflections might seem a bit rhetorical. The present generation of Christians enjoys the dubious claim of dispensing itself from the burden of reading the spiritual classics, and of scarcely reading even third- and fourth-hand writers on spirituality. The great mystics are perceived as being out of date, exaggerated, or unbalanced in their theological and anthropological presuppositions. Ironically, however, it is a known fact that the best contemporary spiritual writers — those who have been or are still widely read — have all restated the teachings and basic experiences of the great mystics through the simple expedient of dressing them in a more contemporary idiom and style.

Obviously, we have to overcome certain problems of cultural sensibility and language interpretation if we want to do justice to the style of the mystics and have access to them for the enrichment of our own Christian experience. We cannot expect Christians who lived four hundred years ago, in a different culture and society, and in an unfamiliar "model" of church — however holy they might be — to share our immediate anxieties, to hold our theological overview, or to work within our social, cultural and anthropological categories. Their whole linguistic outlook has to be different from ours. This is an elementary hermeneutical procedure to be used in approaching any important work of the past, including the Bible. We would not read the New Testament mainly for its notions on society, history or science; rather, we seek the core of Jesus' message and his liberating teachings. Just so when we attempt to interpret the classics of spirituality: We should approach them with our minds set on retrieving from their cultural trappings the gospel values which they lived and wished to share with us, thus discovering that they were trying to live the same ideals that we do, and that they had to face basically the same difficulties, temptations and conflicts.

ONE

The Seduction
of God

"GOD ALONE SUFFICES" — TERESA OF AVILA

Distinctive of all mystics is the quality and intensity of their experience of God. Christian mysticism does not consist in having extraordinary religious experiences; rather, it consists in the authentic living of ordinary religious experience. In this sense, every believer has something of the mystic about him or her, although we tend to reserve the words *mystic* and *contemplative* for those persons whose religious experience—the experience of God—is habitually very intense, authentic and permanent.

In today's spirituality the experience of God is often spoken and written about as a value that emerges concomitantly with some Christian commitment, especially in the context of service to the poor. Now then, the experience of God is a very serious, real and demanding business, and the indiscriminate

25

use of this expression can easily debase it, as has happened in the past with many other fine, Christian words. In fact, contemporary Christianity does not seem to be producing many mystics in the full sense of that term, and that should make us stop and think.

The mystics remind us that the experience of God in history – which we are sincerely searching for today – is something essential to Christian identity. It is an arduous process, with its own special demands. Above all, it is an original and irreducible experience. For the mystics, the experience or contemplation of God – intimacy with God – is something altogether different from any other human or psychological experience. It coexists with life and action but remains undiluted by them and cannot be reduced to any created reality; the God who is experienced is an absolute and irreducible reality, always greater than human beings, and greater than all their projects and actions.

Whenever I read a passage from St. Teresa of Avila, I am convinced that God and the experience of God are as real as any object I can touch, or as any historical event I have witnessed. To read St. Teresa is to perceive that God truly exists as a reality that is present and can be experienced in our life, and not just as a rather convincing idea. To read Teresa or, for that matter, any of the authentic mystics, is to "take a bath in God." At this point, we might well recall the venerable theological proposition that God can be affirmed either by way of reason or by way of experience, and that in this same line of thinking modern philosophers like Bergson have ranked the experience of the mystics as a privileged sort of "proof" for the existence of God.

It has been rightly said that Teresa of Avila did not work out a theology of spirituality (as John of the Cross did), partly because she had no formal training in theology and partly because her style was so unsystematic, personal and spontaneous. More than anything else, Teresa transmitted an experience, which she tried to formulate and objectify as best she could, and this religious experience, because it was so real, so profound and so doctrinal, became in turn a source of spiritual teaching. When we read St. Teresa, we are standing not before some doctrinal discourse but before the reality of God and the experience of God.

This great lover of God, who wrote to her nuns in the same vein, sought after God in the most radical way, not only in the privacy of her cell, but among the daily choices she had to make in the midst of her struggles and trials as a reformer, as well as in the struggle against herself. She knew that "the Lord walks among the pots and pans" (today we would say, more prosaically, that God should be sought and experienced in history and in life), but she also knew how precarious both this search, and her fidelity to it, could be. Her contemplative path was not a primrose path of continual ascents, but was also, like ours, made up of successive conversions, discoveries and, yes, of infidelities and mistakes.

I would like to repeat, however, that the most impressive aspect of her message is that contemplation and mysticism are presented to us as real, attainable experiences which have their own distinctive development and have their own distinctive efficacy. Teresa teaches us that the experience of God is a decisive fact, one that includes the whole gamut of human experiences; that like God himself, this experience has an absolute and determinant value; and that the influence of this experience not only accompanies our struggles and commitments, but also qualifies and radically humanizes them:

> When the soul has reached this state, Martha and Mary always act together, as we may say. For the soul takes its part in outward actions . . . which, when they spring from this root, are lovely, sweet-smelling flowers growing on the tree of a love of

God solely for His own sake, unmixed with self-interest. The perfume of these blossoms is wafted to a distance, blessing many souls, and it is lasting, for it does not pass away without working great good. . . . For truly, as I have seen in several cases, souls raised by God to this state are oblivious . . . of their own loss or gain. . . . They never calculate as to whether they will lose themselves by it, but think about the welfare of others and of nothing else, forgetting themselves for the sake of God in order to please Him better—and they will even lose their lives if need be, as did many of the martyrs . . . (*Conceptions of the Love of God*, Ch. VII, par. 3 and 5).

Today, legitimately, we are looking for an incarnate and historical spirituality that avoids dualisms, especially between the presence of God and the reality of history, between contemplation and action. Teresa of Avila helps us understand that intimacy with God is not a dualistic "pole" to overcome, still less a temptation to escapism, but is rather an essential dimension in the incarnate nature of Christian spirituality. And it is essential not only in the sense that if we lack the experience of the God of Christianity we have nothing to incarnate as witnesses of faith and of the gospel. It is essential also on a deeper and more radical level, because the very God we experience forms part of history and of human realities as their Lord and sustenance, and because he neither reveals himself, nor allows himself to be experienced fully, except within that history and those realities.

The Experience of the One Who We Know Loves Us

For St. Teresa the historical experience of God is summed up and takes place in prayer. In Teresa's synthesis the way of spirituality and of human perfection coincides with the way of prayer. For her, prayer is as much a part of history and human reality as are social and pastoral activities, or indeed, as is any form of productive human work. But among them all, prayer has an eminent value: the value of intimacy with God, the only and absolute Lord. Through her own experience, Teresa knew that this intimacy of prayer as an experience of God is an end and value in itself, but also that it is an indispensable means for attaining our personal liberation since God is the God of life and liberty. Therefore, Teresa affirms that prayer is a matter of life or death for the Christian, that it can never be replaced by anything else, that one must never turn back on the road of prayer, and that there is no other remedy for the lack of prayer than to begin praying once more. In all of her works she constantly harks back to this basic resolve.

Many of us today seem to think that (or rather, act as if) Christian experience and the encounter with God are authentic only when they take place in a context of realistic commitment. We seem to regard prayer as something which, though certainly beneficial, is in practice something marginal, a sort of Christian luxury which we have neither the time nor the inclination to cultivate seriously. We seem not to be troubled whether our prayer habits are authentic or of good quality, whether we are making any progress in them, whether we have any difficulties in prayer, or whether, if some situation is preventing us from praying, we ought to be doing something definite to overcome it.

Teresa's message is an alarm signal to those of us who have lost interest in advancing in prayer or have consigned it to the shadowy margin of our Christian commitments. For Teresa, prayer is a living thing, and like all living things, it is meant to grow. Like all living things prayer can have illnesses and crises that frustrate it, and with it, our whole Christian being. In all her works she is at pains to describe development in prayer, difficulties in prayer and ways of overcoming them, as well as the illusions and blind spots that may beset us along the way. In a well-known passage in her *Life* (Chapters 11-13), Teresa distinguishes four degrees of prayer which she likens to four ways of watering a garden. In the *Interior Castle*, she distinguishes seven degrees of prayer which she likens to seven "Mansions" of the Lord's dwelling in the soul. In *The Way of Perfection*, which is less systematic, she returns to the fourfold distinction of vocal and mental prayer, the prayer of recollection and the prayer of quiet. It is not easy to gather all she has said in these three works into a single synthesis, nor are they always logically compatible with one another. The main point to notice is the coherence which Teresa sees and experiences between the way of prayer and the way of Christian progress.

In doing all this, Teresa is not out to satisfy our curiosity or to boast of her spiritual knowledge. Rather, she wants to convince her readers of the fact that prayer has to be taken seriously, with all its dynamics and laws of growth, and that this requires continuous application and effort. By that very fact she questions those ministries and pastoral forms in which prayer has practically no place, or is taken for granted. It would be of little worth to offer the tools of biblical formation, social analysis and critical awareness to Christian communities and their ministers, if at the same time we did not offer them formation and advancement in prayer, since prayer is nothing else but a "deferred" experience of God, stemming from these very tools of formation, and one without which these tools lose their Christian meaning.

It is the task of evangelization to help people advance in prayer. The people of Latin America have a great capacity for contemplation along simple lines of prayer that are consistent with the Teresian tradition, for prayer "in my opinion is nothing else than an intimate sharing between friends;

it means taking time frequently to be alone with Him who we know loves us" (*Life*, Ch. VIII, par. 5). But this friendship and intimacy is meant to grow and be purified until it becomes fully liberating. This is a difficult undertaking for the majority of people unless they receive some pastoral and spiritual help. I know many people who are truly interested in prayer, and whose prayer is of a high quality. Today, these people often tend to be deeply committed to the welfare of others and to solidarity with the poor. But unless they have the support and guidance of their pastoral leaders, all that God wishes to do through them and their prayer may only reach the halfway mark. In this case, it will not be they, but rather their ministers, who will have to answer to God.

The Prayer of Fidelity

Another value in our contemporary theological and spiritual search derives from the importance we attach to commitment and Christian solidarity, namely, a quest for a synthesis between contemplation and commitment. This concern has its place in the best spiritual tradition of the church and is well represented by the Spanish mystics. St. Teresa leaves us no room for doubt in this matter. For her, true prayer is not only inseparable from true Christian commitment, but is performed in practice and is prepared for and anticipated in fidelity to this practice. "Let the will continue to grow if it is to take advantage of prayer." Prayer is practically impossible without a holy life, conformity to the will of God here and now, and the imitation of Jesus' way of being.

> I insist again: your foundation must not consist of prayer and contemplation alone. Unless you acquire the virtues and practice them, you will always be dwarfs (*Interior Castle*, Seventh Mansions, Ch. 4, par. 9).

31

> Remember, it is of the greatest importance – the sole aim of one beginning to practise prayer should be to work and be resolute and prepare herself with the utmost diligence to conform her own will to the will of God (*Interior Castle*, Second Mansions, par. 9).

We should note that for St. Teresa, Christian commitment or practice coincides with conformity to the will of God, and that this will of God is always present as the Christian's primary task. To speak today of conformity to the will of God may sound pietistic, but in the language of the mystics it is a very demanding reality which goes to the root of our Christian identity in any commitment. In today's world, it is in conformity with God's will that human beings should grow, should have abundant life, and should live together as brothers and sisters. Today, we are "conformed to the will of God" by opting for the poor and for justice.

Popular devotion, for its part, has maintained a strong sense of conformity with the will of God. This is, in fact, the basic reason (there can be others along with it) for people's capacity to accept the suffering and harshness of life without losing faith and hope. We know that this attitude is not without its ambiguities, and that it can lead, at times, to a state of passive resignation and even fatalism. We also know that the gospel attitude of conformity to the will of God calls for purification and continual reinterpretation, insofar as it needs to be stated that God's will is first and foremost the life and integral liberation of the people, and that the best way to become conformed to God's will is to work to achieve this primary goal.

Even so, conformity with the will of God will always have a dimension of acceptance, something that Christian people have not forgotten. Accepting the inevitable, the human condition, one's way of life, suffering and the intransigence of death as conformity to the will of God is still good spirituality.

It is something quite different from simply putting up with it all. It calls for the kind of radical reinterpretation of life that only faith can give. Struggle and acceptance can be equally active and valiant as two different ways of conformity to the liberating will of God.

In putting prayer and Christian action into one and the same experience of God, St. Teresa reminds us that Christian commitment includes a dimension of eternity, of anticipation of the kingdom of heaven, and of nostalgia for the absoluteness of God. She thereby brings us to question and justify the Christian quality of our action, which must be done for the sake of the kingdom of God and which is not limited to any particular commitment or action. The kingdom must be present in our action not only as an anticipation in history (the values of the kingdom which we must sow and make grow in the world), but also for its transcendent and eternal dimension. Christian action already contains an eternal dimension without which it would not be fully Christian. This dimension is guaranteed by prayer and contemplation.

Strange as it may seem, the experience of the mystics reveals to us concretely this tension between the absolute and history, between heaven and human tasks. To live this tension is a guarantee that we have taken both its dimensions seriously, and that we are struggling to bring them into a unity. Let us recall what St. Paul says:

> For, to me, "life" means Christ; hence dying is so much gain. If, on the other hand, I am to go on living in the flesh, that means productive toil for me — and I do not know which to prefer. I am strongly attracted by both; I long to be freed from this life and to be with Christ, for that is the far better thing; yet it is more urgent that I remain alive for your sakes (Phil 1:21-24).

This is not just a personal experience of Paul's; it is the

paradigm of the experience of all contemplatives and of all committed people who are sometimes inwardly emboldened in their always unfinished endeavor to live simultaneously for God and for others. In similar words, St. Teresa shares with us her experience of this same tension between living with Christ and living for others:

> And the greatest thing I offer God as a principal service to Him is that, since it is so painful for me to live separated from Him, I desire to live, but out of love for Him. I should like to live with great trials and persecutions (*Spiritual Relations*, Ch. III).

And in one of her best-known poems, she exclaims: "I die because I do not die . . . Longing to behold you, I desire to die." (John of the Cross has a very similar poem.)

"THE BRIGHT NIGHT" – JOHN OF THE CROSS

An important condition for reading the mystics is that it should be done at the right moment in one's spiritual development. In order to grasp and interpret what they are trying to tell us from their very different linguistic and cultural context, and in order to get the benefit of their experience and message enriched by our own experience and contemporary outlook, we need a certain amount of maturity and wisdom. One arrives at the classics; one doesn't begin with them. In order to appreciate a great tradition, one has to be an adult, at least in spirit. I know people who have rediscovered the great mystics (whom they had read in their initial formation, but abandoned later) after they had gone through many crises and transformations and had traveled a long way in their Christian and pastoral lives. Their re-encounter with the great mystics, far from being a backward step in their journey, was really a sign that they had become mature travelers.

I believe that what I have just said is particularly applicable

in the case of St. John of the Cross. A premature reading
of his works could result in discouragement. His doctrine,
with its heavy stress on the negative, might seem somewhat
dehumanizing. The high mysticism and union with God which
he propounds might seem to be incapable of affecting us now.
Moreover, his language and symbolism might easily strike
us as being beyond our reach. Surprisingly enough, however,
as his writings continue to be better interpreted and purified
of the mutilations they were subjected to by the circumstances
of his times, it turns out that the more we want to renew our
spirituality and live our Christian commitments more radically, the more this holy Carmelite's doctrine seems indispensable. We discover the purity of his biblical categories, the
genial character of his mystical synthesis, and the contemporary relevance of his symbols and his message.

While John is the most cultured and systematic of all the
Spanish mystics, he is not primarily a theologian, but rather
a contemplative and, as such, a poet. As a mystic, he intensely lived his experience of intimacy with God, and the
sole concern of his writings is to help us share in this intimacy and walk the road of union with God's love, which
he called "the dark night of the ascent of Mount Carmel."

The Way of Conversion

If we could simplify Teresian spirituality, we would have
to do so in terms of the doctrine and the path of prayer.
Analogously, if we want to simplify the doctrine of John of
the Cross, we would have to follow the lifeline of the doctrine and path of conversion to God. No other Christian writer
has plumbed the theme of Christian conversion as profoundly
and exhaustively as he has, ranging from the first stages of
the flight from sin, all the way to the "mystical marriage."
In this process, John neglects neither psychology nor anthro-
pology nor external activities. His idea of conversion is thor-

oughgoing and integral: Every faculty and every human structure must be converted to God. John examines this process in all its implications: the conversion of the senses, memory, affections, understanding and will, all of which constitute the core message of his "ascetical" works (*The Ascent of Mount Carmel* and *The Dark Night*), so as to issue into the experience of God, which is the fruit of conversion (*The Spiritual Canticle* and *The Living Flame of Love*).

But there is nothing voluntaristic or anthropocentric about John's itinerary of conversion. The center of his spirituality and his notion of conversion is always the God who has first loved us. His point of departure is the fact that God has been "converted" to us from the outset and wishes to transmit to us his life and total liberation. But this cannot take place so long as we are filled with anything that is incompatible with love, with liberty, or with God. Hence the need for purification (conversion) and the emptying out of all our idols and selfishness so as to allow God to act upon and enter our being and our faculties, to transform them according to his love.

> The reason, as we learn in philosophy, is that two contraries cannot coexist in the same subject. Darkness, an attachment to creatures, and light, which is God, are contraries and bear no likeness toward each other. . . . Consequently, the light of divine union cannot be established in the soul until these affections are eradicated (*Ascent*, Book I, Ch. 4, No. 2).

Hence the need to go through the nights, which are the eclipse of non-love in us, so that God's love may illumine us. Hence, too, the "path of ascent" leads upward through the "nothingnesses" of the uptorn roots of a selfishness that oppresses us and prevents us from loving.

The outcome of this nocturnal path of purification is the illumination of our faith, our hope and our commitment to charity. Christian conversion will always be superficial unless it is grounded in faith, hope and love, which are the virtues that unite us to God and to the service of our neighbor. John's insistence on the value of faith and love, and on the fact that these virtues are primary for conversion, should put us on our guard against those false spiritualities and Christian commitments that are based on values devoid of faith and love. Poverty, solidarity, suffering and chastity are part of Christian spirituality precisely because of the faith, hope and love that they involve and evoke, and not for what they are in themselves alone. The synthesis of John's mystic way may be reduced to this:

The maturity of conversion consists in maturity of faith and love, and fruit of our purifications and "nights" must be that we are brought to live our ordinary life, motivated by faith, hope and love, and not by selfishness, by sensibility or by reason alone. "At the evening of life, you will be examined in love" (*Sayings of Light and Love*, No. 57).

Along this path, faith and love, expressed as contemplation and Christian practice, become but one thing. No other mystic has joined faith and love so indissolubly in both experience and doctrine as John has. In fact, in his spiritual way we cannot discern whether his master idea is the purification of faith or the purification of love:

> We must discuss the method of leading the three faculties (intellect, memory, and will) into this spiritual night, the means to divine union. But we must first explain how the theological virtues (faith, hope, and charity) . . . cause the same emptiness and darkness in their respective faculties: faith in intellect, hope in the memory, and charity in the will. Then we shall explain how in order to journey to God the intellect must be perfected in the darkness of faith, the memory in the emptiness of hope, and the will

in the nakedness and absence of every affection (*Ascent*, Book II, Ch. 6, No. 1).

The Darksome Way

In many discussions on spiritual theology it has been debated whether Christian experience is primarily an experience of faith or the practice of charity and commitment. Whether one opts for the former position (labeled "orthodoxy") or the latter (labeled "orthopraxis"), the whole thing seems rather alien, both to the religious sense of the people and to the teaching of the mystics. For St. John of the Cross, faith is the foundation of love, and love is the soul of faith. The fullness of faith coincides with the fullness of love. Both lead us to a commitment for others and to union with God who humanizes and liberates us.

This doctrine has its lessons for our own generation which tends to slight faith in favor of love, or vice versa. John teaches that faith without love is not Christian faith, but rather a dead ideology, incapable of leading us either to communion with God or to the following of Christ. He likewise teaches us that love without faith is doomed to extinction, partiality or self-serving, since true charity, which is all gift, all gratuitousness, stems from our faith-conviction in the love of the God who dwells within us and is motivated by this faith-conviction and not by mere altruism.

Moreover, in the teaching of St. John of the Cross faith and love are not static attitudes which we possess, without further ado in our spirit. They are essentially dynamic, always undergoing a process of purification: Either they are purified and grow, or else they stagnate and die. Faith is not a deposit; it is a continual search. The same is true of love. We find God to the extent that we seek him in the "ascents" and "nights" of loving faith. God gives himself to us along the "road" that leads to him, and does so in the measure that we travel along that road. This road toward God—which is upward and dark because it purifies us from our idols—is nonetheless a gratifying road, for its night leads us to greater light, and its arduous ascent leads us toward an encounter with our destiny.

The Fertile Desert

In explaining the path to union with God, John joins two great biblical themes which correspond to two experiences of Christian mysticism: union with God as both a struggle and a celebration. In biblical tradition, the theme of struggle—purification, conversion, turning away from idolatry—is symbolized in Exodus, in the prophets and in the desert. The theme of celebration—the presence of and communion with God—is symbolized in the Temple, the Covenant, worship and religious feasts. Both dimensions are essential in Christian spirituality. Both are also liberating: liberation as an exodus from sin and oppression, and as continual conversion and purification (the "desert"); liberation as communion with others in celebrating the gift of God and his covenant of gratuitous love (the "feast").

Struggle and gratuitousness, liberation and communion, are demands not only of the Christian way, but also (and for the same reasons) of the human condition. They are experiences of the Christian people: a people who work, a people who celebrate communion because they know that the total reality of human beings, both in their relationship to God and to others, is much more than a matter of struggles; because they likewise know that the capacity to celebrate God's life and covenant with us is already an experience of liberation. This people can live in the night of suffering and injustice while maintaining the light of their faith and hope in God.

For St. John of the Cross, the vocation and liberation of humankind cannot be achieved without struggling, in the first place, against the slaveries of the world, the flesh and the spirit. Intimacy with God—which is the fulfillment of the human vocation—is attained by dying to evil and to all forms of selfishness. This is one part of his teaching: the struggle to encounter God as a kind of night, of ascent, of negation (the *nadas*). At the same time, the liberating experience of God brings with it the intimacy and joy of nuptials and the fullness of a flame of love. In John's poetic mysticism, night and ascent are symbols of an arduously attained liberation, while nuptials and flame are symbols of deep communion.*

Today we are searching for a spirituality of liberation and a spirituality of communion with different emphases according to the diverse needs of various regions and experiences. In this search, St. John of the Cross reminds us that union with God is the fullness of all values and the paradigm of the human vocation, but that in our historical situation this experience of God also comes to us both as a striving for liberation and as a full and humanizing communion.

In this search for personal liberation as an anteroom to a better relationship (communion) with others, many people would opt today for one or another of the various humanist paths. There are those who hold that the path of liberation from the "demons" which enslave people or impede human communion is to be sought in transforming those social structures that are the source of slaveries, including inner slaveries. Others opt for the path of psychology as the key to liberation of spirit and communion with others. On the one hand, there are those who opt for social revolution; on the other, there are those who opt for psychoanalysis or some other

*We find this symbolism in the overall structure of his writings. The first is referred to in *The Ascent of Mount Carmel* and *The Dark Night;* the second in *The Spiritual Canticle* and *The Living Flame of Love*. On the symbol of nuptials, see *The Spiritual Canticle*, Stanzas XIV-XV, Nos. 2 and 30, and Stanza XXVII ff.

form of psychotherapy. This cultural fact has impregnated vast sectors of contemporary spirituality which—depending on the different types of society in which they arise—tend to define their objectives in terms of sociology or of psychology. Stated in radical terms: In poor countries, there could be no spirituality without a political dimension; in rich countries, there could be no spirituality without a dimension of psychological self-realization. Stating it in even more radical terms: Intimacy with God would seem to be a luxury, a characteristic of people without access to the sciences of society or of the psyche.

The mysticism of St. John of the Cross does not offer us a path that is an alternative or substitute for the human desire to grow, and to grow in communion. But it does put us on the alert against excessive trust in the tendencies of "sociologism" and "psychologism" as regards inner liberation. It does so by reminding us of the primacy of the purification of faith and love, and also of the liberation of the root of human being, which can only be achieved in the search for union with God.

The gospel paradox that death to selfishness (the *nadas*) and the psychological purification of faith and love (the *nights*), which lead to a fulfilling and liberating intimacy with God, cannot be substituted for by any exercise of the human sciences. In Christian spirituality the search for God in faith and love is of the essence, while the help derived from psychology and sociology is complementary. According to John, psychological growth is liberating to the extent that it purifies and liberates faith and love. It is through faith and love— and not through the senses, the memory, or the reason— that we become united with God here on earth. Today's psychologists would have much to gain by getting to know St. John of the Cross.

To put it in yet another way: The most humanizing and

liberating attitudes of the human spirit are not attained by dint of analysis or psychological procedures (although these may help in paving the way), but by the slow action of the Spirit on our spirit in the measure that we are willing to be purified by him and grow in love. Humility, patience, valor and determination are before all else the fruit of this action of God rather than the result of our psychological efforts. In like manner, hunger and thirst for justice and a commitment in solidarity with the suffering and oppressed of this world are not brought about by the mere analysis of social realities or by adherence to an ideology, but rather, by the purification of our selfishness and conformism through the power of Christ and by the transformation of deceitful visions of human reality through the purification of faith. In this process, developing social awareness and conscience is doubtless a help and a tool that should by no means be spurned.

> I should like to persuade spiritual persons that the road leading to God does not entail a multiplicity of considerations, methods, manners and experiences . . . but demands only the one thing necessary: true self-denial, exterior and interior, through surrender of self to suffering for Christ. . . . In the exercise of this self-denial everything else, and even more, is discovered and accomplished (*Ascent*, Book II, Ch. 7, No. 8).

In summary, what John of the Cross would say to us today is really something rather simple and basic, although sometimes, oddly enough, forgotten: Christian spirituality must deal in the first place with God, and not with any kind of creature; that the encounter and experience of God (the fundamental Christian experience) comes essentially through faith; that faith must be continually loved, cultivated and purified, since nothing can take its place; and that faith does not grow through the exercise of any human science but according to its own distinctive way, namely, by denying whatever contradicts faith and by allowing God to purify our faith when he communicates with us.

All these things, which we ordinarily refer to as the experience of God, are a source of radical liberation and constitute the only way in which we can expel the "demons" of human selfishness, since the presence of God is incompatible with the presence of any form of evil or of non-love.

TWO

Christian Realism

The Critical Consciousness of the Mystics

One of the most relevant contributions stemming from the teaching of the great mystics is what we may call their Christian realism. This realism involves the appraisal of an attitude toward human realities and possessions and, in more general terms, toward "creatures." In contemporary language we would say that it involves the appraisal of and attitude toward the body and human psychology, toward the social, cultural and economic goods that shape the human condition. The attitude of the mystics toward these realities is marked by a fundamental conviction: Sin is present in human reality; hence, this reality is ambiguous; but the Spirit of God is likewise present in all these realities; hence, these realities are also ways to God, in the measure that we purify and liberate our faith and our love (mind and heart).

45

The point of departure for this conviction is both realistic and Christian, since it implies a lively awareness of sin in all its forms, and there is no Christian spirituality without a sense of sin. This sense of the reality of sin, both in themselves and in the world, is something of a commonplace in the writings of the mystics ("we are sinners" is never an empty phrase on their lips). The same can be said of their sense and experience of everything that leads to sin (occasions and temptations), as well as the consequences of sin in the life of the individual and the church.

Because we have been formed according to different theological and anthropological criteria, and certainly because the sense of sin in the contemporary world, even among Christians, has begun to undergo an eclipse, the mystics' vision of reality may seem pessimistic to us. As a result, one of the objections frequently leveled against them is their "dualistic" vision of spirituality. It would seem as if God can only be found in prayer, in the word and sacraments of the church, in our soul, in self-denial—and in the cross—but not in external activities or in history or temporal realities. It would seem that "goods" and "creatures," and even the human body, are sources of sin and obstacles to be overcome.

There may be an element of truth in such appraisals, not because these spiritual writers were mystics and saints, but because, despite that fact, they were children of the culture and worldview prevalent in the philosophy of their time. But that is not the point. The essence of the vision of human realities and capacities which we find in the mystics derives not so much from theological or cultural conditioning as it does from their very experience of God. They are neither pessimists nor dualists, but above all, realists.

For them God is a reality. He is the Source-Reality of all other realities; he is the only Reality that is free of sin, ambiguity or imperfection. All other realities are not God;

therefore, they are relative and subject to corruption. It might seem to us that these affirmations, for all their truth, are abstract and inconsequential. But for contemplatives they are an experience of life and are fraught with consequences. Their apparent contempt of the world is really not what it seems. It is rather their conviction of the relativity of everything created and of the absoluteness of God alone, the only trustworthy redeemer of human realities in which his Spirit already dwells. What they are trying to tell us is that no created reality is to be loved above all else; that evil can taint any reality, and that this taint can contaminate us and in fact does contaminate us. The sin which is in us and in society does not come from God or from his will for us, but rather from our inner and outer world. This is neither pessimism nor dualism; it is Christian realism. The sin of the world is an integral part of all reality. The more real our experience of God, the more truly we will experience the reality of this sin and the call to struggle against it both in ourselves and in society.

Teresa's "God alone suffices," John's "all and nothing," and Ignatius' "indifference toward all things created," are not expressions of pessimism or antipathy with regard to human realities; rather, they reflect a great love of God, as well as for his plans for creation which have been lamentably deformed by sin.

To put it in more modern terms, there is no injustice, selfishness or oppression in God, but all of them exist in us and in the reality of our world. Not only that, but the more we love and experience God and his kingdom within us, the more we sense that absence of God which sin is. The more we experience God as the source of liberation and happiness, the more we regard all forms of sin as an evil and a misfortune to be avoided at all costs. The more we know God experientially as the Love who gave and gives himself for us, the more we perceive the un-love of sin and the precariousness of human goods and realities.

> The first and chief benefit that this dry and dark night of contemplation causes is the knowledge of self and of one's own misery (*The Dark Night*, Book I, Ch. 12, No. 2).

For these mystics, sin was a reality they felt as intensely and personally as they felt their experience of God. This explains their acute awareness not only of their own personal sins, but also of the sins of their age. Their sense of sin was realistic. For them sin did not exist in the abstract; it was incarnate in the historical events they experienced.

This is why, in their treatment of Christian spirituality, they stressed the dimension of struggling against evil, against infidelities, and against all forms of seduction. This, too, is why they insisted on watchfulness against the temptations, blindnesses and snares inherent in all human realities. Their call to sacrifice and renunciation regarding these realities is Christian realism.

They know that we can lose God's love, thereby losing ourselves both for God and for others. And they know that this is the only frustration for which there is no remedy.

> The first colloquy is with our Lady, that she may obtain grace for me from her Son and Lord for three things: 1. That I may have a thorough knowledge of my sins and a feeling of abhorrence for them. 2. That I may comprehend the disorder of my actions, so that detesting them I will amend my ways and put my life in order. 3. That I may know the world, and being filled with horror of it, I may put away from me worldly and vain things (*Spiritual Exercises*, First Week, Third Exercise).*

*Also St. Teresa of Avila, *Interior Castle*, First Mansions, Ch. 2, par. 15; Life XXXII, par. 6; also St. John of the Cross, *Ascent*, Book I, Ch. 12; Book II, Ch. 7; etc.

The Renunciation That Generates Love

The importance that these saints attach to abnegation and asceticism, as well as to the acceptance of suffering and disappointments, does not derive, therefore, from some hidden dualism or contempt for the world, although they sometimes use the latter expression. For them the *world* (as used in the fourth gospel) is the sin of their time and the ambiguity of reality as a source of human servitude. The self-denial and asceticism which they firmly taught and more firmly practiced is the only realistic condition for liberating oneself from these servitudes and ambiguities in order to be able to grow in love. Decidedly asceticism and the cross, as represented in their writings, cannot be understood apart from a realistic view of the world and, above all, from a desire to grow in love. Asceticism is a condition and a measure of love; above all, it is the realistic way of imitating the freedom of Jesus before the world and his great and measureless love.

> For my part, I hold that the measure of our power to carry a heavy cross or only a light one is that of our love. Therefore, Sisters, . . . brace yourselves to suffer whatever His Majesty wishes . . . "*Fiat voluntas Tua.*" My Lord, fulfill your will in me in every shape and form that you desire. If you will that it be in trials, give me strength and let them come; if it be in persecutions, dishonors, sickness and need, here I am; I will not turn away my face, my Father, nor is it right that I should flee from them (*The Way of Perfection*, Ch. XXXII, par. 7 and 10).

This realism finds particularly radical expression in the writings of St. John of the Cross. In this connection, his maxims on "all and nothing" are striking:

> Endeavor to be inclined always:
>   not to the easiest, but to the most difficult;
>   not to the most delightful, but to the harshest;

not to the most gratifying, but to the less pleasant;
not to what means rest for you, but to hard work;
not to the consoling, but to the unconsoling;
not to the most, but to the least;
not to the highest and most precious, but to the
     lowest and most despised;
not to wanting something, but to wanting nothing;
do not go about looking for the best of temporal
     things, but for the worst,
and desire to enter for Christ into complete nudity,
     emptiness, and poverty in everything in the
     world. . . .

When you turn toward something
you cease to cast yourself upon the all.
For to go from all to the all
you must deny yourself of all in all.
And when you come to the possession of the all
you must possess it without wanting anything.
Because if you desire to have something in all
your treasure in God is not purely your all (*Ascent*,
     Book 1, Ch. 13, Nos. 6 and 11).

For John of the Cross, abnegation and renunciation are
not a death to values, but rather, to the more subtle forms
of slavery and selfishness that reign in us. These cannot be
uprooted except through renunciation, and through a love
that is greater than our tendency to corrupt the values of
reality by our selfishness and our hankering after self-
aggrandizement.

Since the things of the world cannot enter the soul,
they are not in themselves an encumbrance or harm
to it; rather, it is the will and appetite dwelling within
it that causes the damage (*Ascent*, Book 1, Ch. 3,
No. 4).

In our human condition, there is no other way to reach
the freedom of love than by destroying the tendencies which

enslave it through asceticism and self-denial, which control our love. This spirituality of *nadas* is realistic because it knows that love will not grow if it is not progressively liberated, and because it knows that human realities—the world—will not be in love's service so long as human beings do not use those realities with love. But this freedom of love is not possible unless we put to death whatever lives as un-love in ourselves. This death is what abnegation and Christian asceticism aim at:

> The other is . . . the possession of God through union of love. This is acquired through complete mortification of all the vices and appetites and of one's own nature. . . . What the soul calls death is all that goes to make up the old man. . . . All this is the activity of the old life, which is the death of the new spiritual life. . . . For the soul, like a true daughter of God, is moved in all by the Spirit of God (*The Living Flame of Love*, Stanza 2, Nos. 32-34).

Our Experience of Sin

Although it might sound strange to say so, our Christian generation is very close to this realism of the mystics. We too are critical and apparently pessimistic with regard to human realities. We want a critical, prophetic and counter-cultural church. We aim at the consciousness-raising of the Christian people with regard to the ambiguities, temptations and seductions inherent in the reality that surrounds us. What has changed is the content, language and emphases of our world: Today our vision of the kingdom of God is more social, and the "favorite" sins and servitudes of our generation are those that refer to the sins and servitudes of societies and cultures.

In the concrete, we criticize the prevailing economic reality, the manifold forms by which human beings oppress other human beings, social injustices, abuses of human rights, consumerism, drug addiction, and the degradation of sex and family life. We want to be both critical and aware of the snares and ambiguities of ideologies, and of political and cultural seductions. The media of social communication offer little to make us optimistic about human and worldly realities. Christians of future generations who read what we have written on consumerist society, on sexual morality, on human rights and on the arms race, might well come away with the impression that we had the same attitude of contempt for society (the world) and skepticism toward human realities that we ourselves attribute to the classics of spirituality.

Speaking of this similarity between the mystics' experience of the world and ours, I believe that they have much to say that can help us shape our critical consciousness into a spirituality. They were certainly sensitive to all forms of sin as well as of the dehumanization that sin introduces into our lives and our society. Like us, they had their "favorite" sins (those that were most visible in their times), but their mysticism helped them not to be selective in reacting against those evils, since it made them keenly aware of the essential evil of sin: that the greatest evil of reality is its rejection of God and of the kingdom of life he offers us; that the gravest consequence of sin, including social sin, is that it affects God himself, inasmuch as the experience of God and that of sin are incompatible.

This challenges us. Our Christian generation ought to question itself about its sense of sin and about the dehumanization that sin introduces into our lives and into society. A sense of sin is more than a sense of what is good or bad. The latter is ethics; the former is spirituality. We can be sensitive to the injustices and to the crisis of moral values in our civilization, and even struggle for human rights, and still not have a Christian spirituality so long as we do not integrate into our sensitivity and our struggle the fact of God's love which is offended in his sons and daughters. The gospels do not speak to us of justice simply as a human virtue, but of the justice of the kingdom, the source of which is God, and the violation of which is not just a social injustice, but above all, a sin against God.

The test of our spirituality in this respect is whether we are concerned about all injustices and sins, or only with some of them. The distinctive characteristic of a real sense of sin (which is the dark side of the sense of God) is that it frees us from the conditionings and selectivities imposed by culture and society and enables us to go to the root of evil. There are Christians and Christian publications that are very sensitive to the oppression of the poor and to political persecutions, but are much less sensitive to the oppression of believers or to religious persecutions, or vice versa. There are Christians who are sensitive only to martyrs for justice and the rights of the poor, or vice versa. When it comes to exploitation in connection with salaries, eroticism, the degradation of marriage, or some forms of violence some of us are conscious while some of us are blind.

In this respect Christian consciousness-raising, which is so important in the liberation of the poor, is not simply an exercise in social analysis and criticism, but should lead to a spirituality, an awareness in conscience that the mechanisms and disorders of social injustice are a sin that offends God and prevents the world and the reality that surrounds us from becoming an experience of God and of his kingdom.

Our Struggle Against Evil

We tend to regard the asceticism of the mystics as excessive and to characterize their acute sense of the spiritual life as a combat. We have already pointed out that this has to be interpreted in view of their clear perception of sin and the evil it produces, and in view of their conviction that growth in the love of God is the fundamental good of the human being. Our Christian generation, if it wishes to be logically consistent and draw out the consequences of its critical awareness of the lies and servitudes of society, needs to set a much higher value on asceticism and the struggle against these evils—the "enemies of the soul" in the parlance of the classics.

It is not enough for us to be aware of the fact that consumerism, the materialism of our culture, or the gap between the rich and the poor constitute an evil; rather, we have to do something to avoid being seduced by them and to change this state of things. Today we need to practice asceticism and struggle against evil in order to live in keeping with our Christian identity and in order to be agents of change. This seems obvious, but it requires abnegation and asceticism. It is useless to criticize a consumerist society unless we ourselves consume less—and this entails austerity and voluntary poverty. It is useless to deplore the plight of the poor unless we enter into solidarity with them—and this involves many renunciations and contradictions. It is useless to speak of liberation unless we become aware of the fact that every form of human liberation must pass through the renunciations and deaths of selfishness which are involved in overcoming our own servitudes and those of others—modern versions of the *nadas* of St. John of the Cross.

Surprisingly, we have come by way of the human and social sciences to the same conclusion the mystics reached by way of their spiritual experience; namely, that reality is ambiguous, that evil and its seductions are a fact and a permanent temptation, and that in view of all this, we must struggle to become liberated. This is our asceticism. It is present in our affirmations about liberation, in our statement that social liberation and inner liberation go hand in hand, in other words, that justice and asceticism go hand in hand. This same statement is implicit in the teaching of the mystics. St. Teresa, for example, not only had a deep sense of sin as the greatest of evils, but likewise had an awareness of our social responsibility: Between our sins and the evils of our society (or the evils of the church in her day), there is a deep relationship. In her teaching, the reason why the world is not better is that we Christians (and she was thinking of consecrated Christians in particular), are not holier.

Our Christian realism, like that of the mystics, is nothing more than the result of a Christian vision and evaluation of reality which transcends the optimism-pessimism polarity and provides the foundation for the only viable form of humanism. In the spiritual tradition of Christianity, the balance between humanism and abnegation, between the acceptance of worldly values and the renunciation of the world, between progress and austerity, has always posed a problem. The experience of the mystics and our own experience regarding the development and human advancement of peoples has been leading us toward similar conclusions. Today we are increasingly skeptical about those forms of social and material progress that do not involve austerity and renunciation because we can see that they dehumanize people and lead to worse selfishness and injustice. We distrust the growth of societies in power and wealth because we see that power and wealth blind us to the ambiguities and sins that they generate.

The failure of development projects fostered by capitalist and collectivist groups alike, as well as the dehumanizing results they have produced, leads us to think that even on the social, economic and cultural levels there is no real human development (liberation) without a collectively embraced asceticism, renunciation and austerity. Today, we have secularized these terms, but the experience of the mystics, that humankind cannot develop as such without renouncing and breaking with the world, has shown itself to be true.

Christian humanism is based on the premise that humankind is more than human, and that, in order to become such, humankind must struggle against the seductions which invite it to become less than human.

THREE

The Practice of Effective Love

SAINT TERESA AND THE PRACTICE OF FRATERNITY

One emphasis of the spiritual theology emerging in our churches today is its identification of Christianity as the practice of justice, charity and liberation, in other words, as Christian praxis. It insists on the fact that love should be an effective service toward the improvement of human realities, and in particular, that it should take the form of a service and preferential option for the poor. This theological-spiritual stress has been formulated as a re-valuation of orthopraxis in Christian life, a counterbalance to a Christianity and a spirituality that gave too much pride of place to orthodoxy. Christianity means practicing the truth of the gospel, not just believing in it.

These concerns of present-day Christianity amount to a recovery of a vital tradition stemming from the 16th-century mystics. These mystics can also help us understand the place of orthopraxis in spirituality, and the profound value of the practice of effective love in Christianity.

The mystics make no secret of their explicit adherence to the Truth, and to the truths which the church teaches. In an age when this truth was being questioned by various Reformation movements, they made their explicit option for church teaching a vital part of their spirituality, an expression of their fidelity to God. All of them gladly submitted their writings to the authority of the church — despite the obstacles and contradictions that this involved at that time. Nevertheless, their spirituality did not focus on apologetics or on speculations concerning the truth, but rather on the effective practice of love. In doing so, they achieved a great degree of balance which enabled them to overcome both the aridity of a Scholastic theology that had become divorced from the spirituality of the people and from pastoral practice, and the anti-intellectual and a-theological tendencies of the Illuminati, of psuedo-mystics and of certain currents in the *Devotio Moderna*.

For St. Teresa of Avila, the essence of sanctity lies in the practice of conformity with the will of God. We have already noted that, for her, prayer and contemplation both lead to and presuppose this practice of conformity, and that, to her way of thinking, the value of prayer does not derive from the thought or reasonings that accompany it, but rather from the love with which it is made and the practice of love to which it leads.

The Teresian notion of conformity with the will of God basically consists in the effective practice of fraternal love, motivated by the fact that Christ lives in others.

> True perfection is the love of God and of our neighbor. . . . To my way of thinking, the surest sign that we are keeping these two commandments

is that we have a genuine love for others (*Interior Castle*, First Mansions, Ch. 2, par. 17; Fifth Mansions, Ch. 3, par. 9).

This fraternal love involves two mutually inclusive demands: solidarity with and abnegation for the sake of others, and reconciliation and forgiveness in the face of offenses. On these two points, Teresa of Avila is utterly unbending. And these also happen to be the two points in which she addresses our present Christian concerns.

We too are searching for a spirituality that will lead us to practice solidarity with the poorest of the poor (since Christ lives in them in a special way) and to upbuild a new way of living together that is just, fraternal and forgiving. The teaching of St. Teresa not only provides us with a mystique for doing so she reminds us, too, of the irreplaceable worth of forgiveness in the struggle for justice and fraternity. In joining together solidarity and forgiveness, she not only makes forgiveness an important aspect of solidarity but reminds us that the best struggle for fraternity is the one that is undertaken with a reconciled heart.

Humility and Poverty

In this same context, Teresa rescues one more evangelical demand from the oblivion to which it is frequently consigned: the virtue and value of humility. It is well known that, for her, humility is the *experienced* conviction of the truth about God and about our own reality. The truth about God and ourselves is translated into humility when we contrast the gifts God has given us and the misery of our fidelity in response to these gifts. This prevents us from considering ourselves greater than others, and shows us the hollowness of any presumption on our part. This attitude is the path that leads us to overcome selfishness and enables us to become

59

brothers and sisters in solidarity and forgiveness, since we ourselves are the permanent recipients of God's pardon and mercy.

Along these same lines, St. Teresa points out two failures against humble love that were dangerously common in the ecclesial world she knew: seeking the recognition and esteem of others, and what she calls points of honor. A *pundonor* is a feeling of self-worth that leads us to resentment toward others because it seems to us that they do not regard or treat us with sufficient respect. This destroys fraternity and humble love, especially in community life. Teresa's insistence on this point is the result of her own experience in the church and in religious life.

This almost naturally leads Teresa to formulate another demand that is indispensable for the practice of fraternity: detachment and poverty. In this perspective the praxis of poverty as freedom from things, goods, honors, prestige and persons is a consequence of humility, because humility also shows us the truth about worldly realities and their true relation to ourselves. Moreover, poverty, like humility, is a necessary condition for the practice of fraternal love and solidarity because it eliminates the spirit of competition, of envy and of the passion to possess.

> Do not imagine, my sisters, that the things I shall recommend you to practice are many . . . I will confine myself to three points . . . The first is the love we ought to have for one another; the second, detachment from all created things; the third, true humility, which though mentioned last, is the principal virtue, and embraces all the others (*The Way of Perfection*, Ch. IV, par. 4).

The Teresian trilogy of humilty-poverty-fraternity, as the underlying attitude and condition of her Christian practice, coincides with the most important spiritual tradition of the

Middle Ages: Franciscanism. The fundamental value in Francis' spirituality was not, as is commonly said, poverty, but fraternity. His insistence on the poverty and humility of Jesus stems from the fact that he (like Teresa later) understood and experiences that the praxis of effective love is impossible without a profound detachment and a profound humility. And, we might add, because even more than Teresa, Francis perceived that the church of his time urgently needed to reform itself in the practice of poverty, so that it could begin from there its renewal and its conversion to the evangelization of the poor.

On this point as in other aspects of spirituality, the Spanish school incorporates the best of the medieval tradition, represented in this case by St. Francis of Assisi.

ST. IGNATIUS AND THE PRACTICE OF COMMITMENT

The essence of Ignatian spirituality is an interior freedom that leads to the service of Christ and his kingdom. The best systematic treatment of this spirituality, the *Spiritual Exercises*, consists of a process of discernment and of reorientation of our freedom so as to allow us to make an option for the kingdom of Christ, a discernment made in the light of Christ's life, in order to help us know and put into practice God's will for us. For Ignatius, discernment is conversion; it is an option of love; it is the root of Christian commitment and practice.

Ignatian mysticism is a mysticism of commitment, commitment for the kingdom of Christ, that is, a commitment to doing good to others and improving the state of things. In contrast to the caricatures and distortions introduced into his spirituality by later generations, St. Ignatius was a mystic whose outlook had nothing of the rigorist or the rationalist about it. His life commitment, as well as the religious order he founded, cannot be understood merely as a response to or strategy against the Protestant Reformation, but must be seen above all as a service to the kingdom in order to improve the state of things in his time. There are no polemics or allusions to Protestantism in his writings. His central concern was the situation of the church, which was in need of renewal, and the lot of his brothers and sisters in this world. There was nothing politico-religious about the apostolic endeavors he was most directly involved in during the first years of the Society. Rather, his was a commitment to prisoners, to the sick, and to the poorest people of Venice and Rome. For Ignatius, conversion to the kingdom, made in the light of the life of Christ, was a service to the neediest and most abandoned of his brothers and sisters.

The spiritual methods that Ignatius propounds in his *Spiritual Exercises* (meditation, examen, discernment of spirits, and so forth) are meaningful only in the measure that they help Christians grow in the freedom of love. These methods are always relative and flexible, and Ignatius himself did not always follow them exactly. His teaching on obedience, about which so much ink has been spilt, is aimed at assuring freedom and availability for commitment to the kingdom in loyal adherence to the church. He personally lived obedience with a great freedom of spirit; he did not dodge ecclesiastical conflicts as he worked to advance the cause of whatever he thought was best for the kingdom of God. In his spirituality St. Ignatius succeeded in creating a synthesis which is still valid today, joining the best of the medieval tradition and the humanism of the emerging new world with the latter's emphasis on liberty, inwardness and human achievements. This synthesis merges contemplation and practical commitment, fidelity and freedom, mystical experience and realistic psychology.

Ignatian mysticism is a point of arrival in the long journey of medieval spirituality in search of a synthesis between contemplation and commitment. In this connection it represents a complement to the achievement of the Carmelite mystics, whose spirituality is more related to the demands of the contemplative life. But Ignatius is equally representative of Renaissance spirituality in the sense that he belonged to the generation that "discovered" the inner, psychological world of the human being (the modern "inwardness"). Hence, his spirituality is also an excellent synthesis between mysticism and psychology. In this respect he shares with St. John of the Cross the claim of being the father of modern spirituality, with its awareness that the life of faith and love are closely linked with the maturity and purification of the psychological organism.

As a founder, he minimized neither orthodoxy nor theology. Although he held Scholasticism in high esteem, he did not allow himself to fall into the trap of separating theological discourse from love or the practice of charity. His spirituality is dynamic and committed, but it never takes the love of God for granted, as sometimes happens in our generation. For Ignatius, this love is achieved; one must acquire it by dint of daily struggle. It is not merely presupposed. It would be illusory if it were not accompanied by Christian commitment and practice.

> The first point is that love ought to be manifested in deeds rather than words (*Spiritual Exercises*, Fourth Week, "Contemplation to Attain Divine Love").

The Ignatian synthesis between the contemplation of God's love on the one hand, and commitment on the other, is also based on his notion of the indivisibility of love: We cannot divide ourselves between Christ and the world. Here St. Ignatius agrees with Carmelite mysticism in which the idea of the indivisibility of our love for God is also very prominent.

But whereas Teresa and John stress the indivisibility of love as union with God, Ignatius, who is more concerned with contemplation in action, stresses the indivisibility of love as a total and indivisible option for the kingdom of Christ. For Ignatius, the praxis of the kingdom is the measure of our love for Jesus:

> Christ our Lord . . . calls and says: "Whoever wishes to come with Me must labor with Me, so that following Me in suffering, he may also follow Me in glory" (*Spiritual Exercises*, Second Week).

Ignatius' emphasis on Christian practice is sometimes reminiscent of á Kempis' *Imitation of Christ*, which was without doubt one of the most influential books he read during his mystical experience at Manresa. The *Imitation* is representative of the reaction of the *Devotio Moderna* against the idealism and intellectualism of late Scholasticism, as well as a treatise on Christian praxis:

> I would rather feel contrition than know how to define it. . . . Oh, if they were as earnest in uprooting vices and planting virtues as they are in mooting questions, there should not be so many evils in the world and scandal among the people. . . . It often happens that many, although they hear the word of God, feel little inclined to follow it, because they have not the spirit of Christ. . . . What does it profit you to have profound knowledge and argue about the Holy Trinity, if you lack humility and thereby displease the Holy Trinity? . . . If I knew the whole Bible by heart, and all the teachings of the philosophers, what would that profit me without the love of God and His grace? (*Imitation of Christ*, Book I, Ch. 1 and 3).

PROPHETISM IN SERVICE OF THE KINGDOM

The service of the kingdom is the point at which the great

mystics of the 16th century converge in their presentation of the ideal practice of effective love. All of them assumed responsibility in facing the history and needs of their time, and responded to them with a lucid and faithful Christian practice. In this respect they were prophets, and their service of the kingdom was not ordinary, but prophetic. A prophet is a person who discerns the signs of the times in order to undertake the attitude and the response which the Spirit wills. Prophetism is an eminent form of the practice of effective charity.

In the context in which they lived, their historic response to the needs of the kingdom of God was very closely linked to the needs of the church. They lived in the culture and society of Christendom where the idea of the kingdom was practically identified with the idea of the church, where human problems regularly included a religious problematic, and where the most predominant sign of the times for the Christian conscience was the reform of the church. In the face of this challenge, the mystics undertook a clearly prophetic commitment.

Ignatius, Teresa and John of the Cross have the same attitude and the same prophetic practice: to join extreme fidelity and adherence to the church with a practice featuring not words or criticisms, but rather, daring and significant deeds aimed at reforming the church from within. Their prophetism also manifests itself in their distrust in resorting to temporal means and powers and in their insistence above all on evangelical conversion and on the personal and collective holiness of the church. St. Ignatius, whom some later, very superficial critics portrayed as a politician (in the sense that he had been led by quite temporal criteria in his initiatives for the Society) was in fact nothing of the kind. His most important initiatives had to do with the evangelization of the poor and of non-believers in America and the Far East, and the first Jesuit universities were in fact founded in places that were not centers of power (Goa, Sicily and Alcalá).

Because the prophetism of these mystics was genuine, it was linked to the conviction that, if we are to contribute to the reform of the church, we must begin with our own personal reform and sanctification, since there is a close relationship between the holiness of the church and the holiness of its members. Moreover, there is a close relationship between the holiness of the church in its members, and the salvation and sanctification of the world.

In contrast to the criticism usually leveled against the spiritual masters of the past—that their spirituality was focused on individual salvation and sanctification—the three great mystics we have been considering could not separate personal sanctification from a commitment to the kingdom (in the Ignatian school) or personal sanctification from the coming of the kingdom for others (the Carmelite school). They were of course concerned with their own salvation and sanctification, which is a perfectly legitimate Christian concern. Yet this concern is precisely what led them to understand that there is no better way of becoming identified with Christ than to be committed to the service of the kingdom and to mission. Our three mystics began their search for God in their monastic cells in Avila or in the cave at Manresa, and they ended by searching for him along the roadsides of the world, in their numerous foundations and in their missionary ventures —not excluding their personal desire to do missionary work in the Americas and in the Far East.

The three saints we are concerned with also experienced the conflicts and sufferings inherent in Christian prophetism, particularly the misunderstandings and contradictions that the Carmelites had to bear, and the difficulties and obstacles which the Roman authorities put in the way of the Jesuits. None of them had an easy task in bringing about the approval or acceptance of the reforms and vision of the religious life he or she wanted to bring about – and which time would show to have been so necessary.

The most dramatic case was that of John of the Cross. He was imprisoned for nine months for religious and disciplinary reasons and died in disgrace in the eyes of a powerful sector of his own Order. He is one of the saints who have been genuinely persecuted by their own brethren, and his writings were under a cloud of suspicion during an epoch when mysticism and his theology of faith and the cross (two pillars of his spirituality) were regarded by many as smacking of Protestantism. Yet, with the same prophetic equilibrium as Teresa and Ignatius displayed, John did not flinch in his resolve to place his synthesis and spiritual reform at the service of the church, a reform that involved a process of both breaking away and moving forward, yet in continuity with the church, such as it was. The Spanish mystics are the best representatives of the Catholic Reform because they worked out a new synthesis of Christian spirituality which embodied the best tradition of the past yet included those very values which the church of their age had lamentably neglected.

In this context of Catholic prophetism, St. Ignatius of Loyola was the most influential reformer. He conceived his service to the kingdom as a universal commitment and undertaking. His mystical experience at Manresa, which transformed him from a fervent Christian into a man of the church, led him to commit himself to the kingdom of Christ with a loyalty similar to that which he, his father and his forbears for two hundred years had offered through their military service to the kings of Castile. He conceived a new style of life consecrated to the service of the kingdom, thus opening the way for the new congregations of active missionary life that were yet to come. He retained the best traditions of Eastern and Western monasticism (Ignatius studied the Rules of St. Basil and St. Benedict), but included them in a new synthesis which provided a Christian response to the challenges of history: contemplation in action; poverty and obedience in relationship to mission; apostolic creativity and daring (missions in America, China and the Indies), together with communion with and loyalty to the visible church.

The prophetic practice of the Spanish mystics has a relevant message for present-day Christians. Like them, we are aware of both the signs of the times which challenge us as a church, and some of the responses we have to offer. Like them, we realize that the church needs creativity and renewal. But today, perhaps, we are not as conscious as they were of the fact that every reform is in vain unless the reformers are themselves renewed; that it is impossible to separate our Christian commitments from our Christian holiness; that renewal is not achieved by speaking, writing, criticizing or acting outside of the church as it is, but rather, that it is brought about from within the ecclesial communion with liberty of spirit, accepting the contradictions and persecutions involved in our service to the kingdom.

FOUR

Christian Discipleship and the Humanity of Jesus

A Meeting Place Between Mysticism and Popular Devotion

One of the most productive themes in contemporary spirituality is the following of Christ under the promptings of the Holy Spirit. This, in turn, has led to a stress on the humanity of Jesus, the Jesus of history and the Christ of the gospels as the model of Christian practice and the source of inspiration for Christian living.

The knowledge, contemplation and following of the humanity of Jesus has led to a purification of a formerly popular spirituality which featured a distant and sometimes dehumanized Christ. It has also provided a better theological and spiritual foundation for the apostolate, for the option on behalf of the poor, and for the other commitments undertaken by present-day Christians. They can now perceive the similarities and analogies between the historical-social context in which Jesus carried out his mission and the contemporary situations and challenges which they have to face, and can therefore more easily discern, in the practice and attitudes of Jesus, a model to inspire them. The humanity of Jesus is becoming closer and more vital for the Christian people, "who are searching for the ever-new face of Christ, who is the response to their legitimate aspirations for an integral liberation" (*Puebla Document*, No. 173)

This re-valuation of the humanity of Christ should come as no surprise; it has always been a constant factor during great moments in the renewal of the church and, in particular, of Christian spirituality. In our popular tradition the humanity of Jesus has played a most important role from the very outset although in time, mainly through a lack of evangelization, various deformations were introduced. To be convinced of the popularity of the humanity of Christ, one need only recall how open the Christian people have been to devotions to the crib, the passion, the way of the cross, and Christ crucified. This seed is still present and available to us as a basis for evangelization and as a potential generator of a contemporary spirituality. The Christian experience of St. Teresa, St. John of the Cross and St. Ignatius cannot be rightly understood unless we grasp the central place that the humanity of Christ held in it. Here, too, they have much to tell us for the enrichment and profit of our spirituality.

Saint Teresa: The Agony of Christ

St. Teresa writes in her *Life* that one of the most deplorable mistakes in her practice of prayer during the first part of her religious life was to think that meditation and contemplation on the humanity and life of Jesus was only for beginners, and that as one advanced in prayer one should leave behind this "sensible support." In this matter, she later reproached her confessors for their lack of wisdom.

This doing without the humanity of Jesus as the nourishment of her prayer left Teresa unsatisfied, and when she changed confessors she recovered her peace of soul. The spiritual guides she had from that time on confirmed her insight that it was a dangerous illusion to abandon the contemplation of the historical life of Christ—even in the highest degrees of the mystical life—since the humanity of Jesus always remains the only way of access to God and to the demands of his kingdom.

This trying experience in her spiritual life, together with the eminently Christocentric influence of Ignatian mysticism which she received through her Jesuit confessors, led Teresa to stress the capital importance of meditation and contemplation on the life of Christ, and above all on his passion. For her, devotion to the passion of Christ was irreplaceable, since experience had shown her that it provided the most effective and realistic antidote against false mysticism and transformed the mystical life into an imitation of Christ in concrete life:

> I could only think about Christ as He was as man.
> . . . The soul can place itself in the presence of Christ
> and grow acccustomed to being inflamed with love
> for His sacred humanity. . . . This is an excellent
> way of making progress, and in a very short time
> (*Life*, Ch. IX, par. 6; Ch. XII, par. 2; cf. Ch. XIII,
> par. 22).

In the humanity of Jesus, Teresa of Avila encountered the guarantee of balance and realism in Christian contemplation.

In *The Way of Perfection* Teresa likewise confesses that the gospels were the source of her sustenance in prayer, and were practically the only book she used. Her love for Jesus and her desire to follow and imitate him were the central motivation of her life and the only value that concerned her. Even in her most exalted mystical experiences, she valued above all the intimacy with Jesus Christ that they brought her. This love for Jesus and imitation of his life were also the commonest motivation she employed with her sisters in Carmel when she wanted to help them understand the demands of radical poverty of life, of fraternal love, of chastity and singleness of heart. She was continually encouraging them to be "friends of Jesus" and "lovers of Christ."

In our spiritual experience in Latin America (as happens in all Christian experience according to the time and place in which it evolves), in connection with our relationship with the humanity of Jesus we accord pride of place, and rightly so, to certain characteristic devotions: Jesus' predilection in dealing with the poor and the oppressed; the opposition and persecution borne because of his message and missionary practice; his commitment to the kingdom; his prophetism. Surely St. Teresa, if she were living today, would have some of these same devotions, but she would still cherish most dearly and deeply the devotion to the passion of Christ. In this respect, she came closest to popular devotion, in which devotion to the passion is a deep-rooted value of great potential. I believe that there is a message in this for us: Our devotion to the practice of Jesus should not be allowed to eclipse our devotion to the passion of Jesus because it is in his passion and death that the commitment of Jesus reaches the extreme limit of martyrdom. And it is here, too, that his love becomes mysteriously radical and is transformed into a source of hope for the abandoned. The persecution, passion and martyrdom of Jesus will always be the most radical model of our Christian commitment, as well as the cost of our Christian discipleship.

It is true, of course, that devotion to the passion can become deformed. One such deformation consists in isolating the passion and the cross not only from the resurrection, but also from the rest of the active life of Jesus and from his lifelong fidelity to the cause of the kingdom. The devotion to the passion thus becomes a passive value in Christian commitment, which explains why our generation has tended to distrust suffering-oriented devotions. St. Teresa and the great mystics can help us to restore the passion to its proper context in the following of the total life of Christ, and to rediscover the special grace and power for conversion that meditation on the passion can bring, as well as its inspiration for Christian commitment—even to the extent of suffering persecution and martyrdom which are not unknown in our experience. If today there is a need for a spirituality that will prepare us for the demands of martyrdom, we should remember, with St. Teresa, that meditation on the passion is an indispensable component of a life motivated by the gospel.

Saint John of the Cross: The Spirit of Christ

In the spiritual theology of St. John of the Cross, the way of spirituality is a process of purification from sins and vices and a tearing-up of the very roots of self-love until we reach our full humanization in union with God. He calls this process the "nights" of the senses and of the spirit. For those who wish to set out on this way—which is the only one possible in Christian spirituality—John begins by reminding them of the first demand of this process: the decision to follow and imitate humanity of Jesus.

> First, have a habitual desire to imitate Christ in all your deeds by bringing your life into conformity with His. You must then study His life in order to know how to imitate Him and behave in all events as He would (*Ascent*, Book 1, Ch. 13, No. 3)

73

The contemplation and following of Jesus remains as the fundamental and decisive point of reference throughout John's teaching and as his basic criterion for the discernment of spirits and of holiness. John of the Cross analyzed and experienced the highest ways of mysticism, but he was always skeptical of any extraordinary grace or prayer-experience that lacked the realism of the imitation of the life of Christ. Thus he goes so far as to state:

> God values in you an inclination to aridity and suffering for love of Him more than all possible consolations, spiritual visions, and meditations (*Sayings of Light and Love*, No. 14).

On this point John's Christocentrism is radical, and he will accept no religious experience, however good and consoling it seems to be, if it substitutes any other model for that of Jesus.

> A person who has no other goal than the perfect observance of God's law and the carrying of the cross of Christ . . . will bear within himself the true manna (which signified God) . . . (*Ascent*, Book I, Ch. 5, No. 8).

> Never take a man for your example in the tasks you have to perform, however holy he may be. . . . But imitate Christ, who is supremely perfect and supremely holy, and you will never err (*Maxims and Counsels,* "Maxims on Love," No. 78).

> Do nothing nor say any notable word that Christ would not have done or said were He in the state I am, as old as I, and with the same kind of health (*Maxims and Counsels*, "Degrees of Perfection," No. 3).

> If you desire to be perfect, sell your will, give it to the poor in spirit, come to Christ in meekness and

humility, and follow Him to Calvary and the sepulcher (*Maxims and Counsels,* "Other Counsels," No. 7).

This teaching of St. John of the Cross is of great importance for contemporary spirituality, in which we find a number of movements and trends that are characterized by a reevaluation of the mystics, of the gifts of the Holy Spirit in prayer, and of the charisms of the Spirit in Christian life. In the churches of America these trends are to be found in many prayer groups. How are we to evaluate these movements in general, and these prayer groups in particular? The great Carmelite mystic offers us an invaluable and decisive tool for Christian evaluation: the imitation of Christ's commitment in life. In his spiritual doctrine neither the gift of tongues, nor healing, nor collective experiences (however moving or extraordinary) are valid criteria for determining either the divine quality of contemplation, or the degree of faith and charity which the latter presupposes and produces.

> The journey, then, does not consist in recreations, experiences, and spiritual feelings, but in the living, sensory and spiritual, exterior and interior death of the cross (*Ascent,* Book II, Ch. 7. No. 11).

St. John of the Cross knows perfectly well that the only realistic criterion for Christian evaluation—one which, on the one hand, is not subject to illusion or blindness and, on the other corresponds to the incarnate nature of Christian faith and love— is the practice of the following of Christ to the cross. For him, the graces of prayer and the spiritual life have no value in themselves, and the Christian should not become attached to them, because they are not God but only imperfect approaches to him. The only valid way to union with God is through naked faith and willing love of God in conformity with the law of Christ.

> I have said that Christ is the way and that this way
> is a death to our natural selves in the sensory and
> spiritual parts of the soul. . . . For He is our model
> and light. . . . [Thus] the true spiritual person might
> understand the mystery of the door and the way
> (which is Christ) leading to union with God (*Ascent*,
> Book II, Ch. 7, Nos. 9 and 11).

John helps us find an adequate place for the action of the
Holy Spirit. Since the Spirit who dwells in us (and expresses
himself in our prayer and charisms) is the very same Spirit
who dwelt in Jesus during his earthly life and led him to the
radical practice of the Father's will, then the fruit of the action of this Spirit in us will always and only consist in leading
us to imitate Christ's own practice of fidelity to the Father
and to the kingdom. The Spirit who is in us and in the community is always the Spirit of Christ, that is, he tends always
to incarnate faith and love in the manner of Christ. The
charisms of the Spirit cannot be separated from the imitation of the humanity of Jesus.

Moreover, in the Blessed Trinity, the Holy Spirit per-
sonifies, the love and self-gift of the Father and of the Son,
and therefore, God's self-gift to humanity. In the world and
in each human being the Spirit creates a dynamism of obla-
tion which is perfectly expressed in the humanity of Jesus.
Hence, no devotion or experience of the Spirit, whether it
be in prayer, charisms, ministries or in any other form of
activity, can be authentic unless it is expressed as a self-
surrender for others.

Saint Ignatius: The Following of Christ

We have already called attention to the Christocentric
character of Ignatian mysticism as well as to its influence
on all later mysticism, beginning with that of St. Teresa. The
Spiritual Exercises, which are the written synthesis of Igna-

tian spirituality, are essentially a contemplation of the humanity of Jesus in the most significant moments of his life in order to acquire "an intimate knowledge of our Lord, who has become man for me, that I may love and follow Him better" (*Spiritual Exercises*, Second Week).

For St. Ignatius the Christian life means making an option for Christ and serving him in his church. Hence he discourages those who have not made a decision to follow Christ and accept his demands from making the *Spiritual Exercises*. At most, he advises them instead to make only the First Week of the *Spiritual Exercises*, which is devoted to conversion from sin, and to the reorientation and discernment of one's life. He regards the topics of the First Week as simply the principle and foundation for being able to follow Jesus.

The real crisis of the *Spiritual Exercises* comes during the Second Week, with its meditations on the life of Jesus, especially on his active life in service of the kingdom. Here the objective is to bring one to make an option for Christ and his cause. This option to follow Christ—and for Ignatius *following* means serving the kingdom—is motivated by a loving contemplation of the life of Jesus. In order to follow and serve Christ one must seek to encounter him by way of the heart. Therefore the *Spiritual Exercises* are not mainly aimed at exercising logic and reason, but rather at the kind of contemplation and affection that will lead us to love and the will to imitate.

This note is sounded more clearly during the last two weeks. The Third Week, which dwells on the passion, is a contemplation of what constituted the greatest proof of Jesus' love: his martyrdom for us. Here the objective is to deepen our option for Christ until we reach the point of being ready to suffer and die for him and for his kingdom—which is the greatest proof of following him.

> True spirit leads to imitating the Passion of Christ. . . our insulted and despised Lord. . . .
>
> In order better to imitate Christ our Lord and to become actually more like Him, I desire and choose poverty with Christ poor, rather than riches; reproaches with Christ laden with them, rather than honors; and I desire to be accounted as worthless and a fool for Christ, who was first held to be such, rather than wise and prudent in this world (*Spiritual Exercises*, Second Week).

This could just as easily have been written by St. John of the Cross.

Once more we find, in the contemplation and imitation of the suffering humanity of Christ, a vital point of convergence among the Spanish mystics as well as a meeting place between them and traditional popular devotion. But what Ignatius has to say to the spirituality of our generation is that devotion to the passion should lead to an option to follow Jesus and a commitment to extend his kingdom. In St. Ignatius the devotion to the passion is not consolation amid sufferings or a passive identification with the suffering Christ, but it is above all an incentive to follow Jesus radically and to struggle for his kingdom. This is the criterion of Christian fidelity, and a call to an even greater option and love.

FIVE

Christian Liberation

Spirituality and Liberation

For many Christians in the Americas the gospel motivation is a significant component in the struggle for justice and for the rights of the poor and the oppressed. Non-Christians too are aware of the important contribution that Christian mysticism can bring to the long march toward liberation and justice. This spirituality—because of Jesus and his gospel—is, and in many cases has been, capable of motivating Christians to endure sufferings, manifold persecutions and even death in the cause of the justice of God's kingdom. This dimension of spirituality also forms part of contemporary Christian experience.

This is not something entirely new in the Christian tradition of the Americas. Since the first evangelization of the New World in the 16th century, there have been precedents in several of its countries of persecution for the sake of Christ. What is perhaps new in this case is that Christian experience in the service of justice, whatever the consequences might be, is a more conscious commitment today and has created a spiritual theology.

Do the great mystics of the 16th century have anything significant and worthwhile to offer today to this spiritual search? Decidedly so, at least as regards the deep spiritual motivations and evangelical demands required in order to transform commitments for libertion and justice into an experience of faith and Christian love.

Obviously it would be foolish to expect the spiritual masters of the 16th century to have had experiences like our own in the way of concrete commitments and explicit statements on the option for the poor or for liberation and social justice. However, they can—implicitly—teach us a good deal more than might appear at first glance. The mystics were children of their own age. They were born and lived at a time when sociology, economics and political science were unknown; when there was a different conception (even theologically) of poverty and social relationships; when social justice problems were on a very small and regional scale and were resolved in a rather guild-like fashion. There was little awareness of the structural problems of society or analysis of their causes. Charity and Christian mercy were the most effective responses to various forms of human servitude. The ills of the souls and the slaveries of sin were perceived with much greater attention than we accord them today.

In this context, however, the mystics can still serve to remind us of certain values that are essential for the spirituality of liberation; the indissoluble relation between interior liberation and social liberation; the need for a mysticism of faith and love in liberation; the value of poverty and austerity in the building of a more just and fraternal society; the awareness of a God who is both liberated and capable of liberating.

To Liberate, We Must Be Liberated

A spirituality for liberation presupposes both a practice and a mystique. The practice of liberation is manifold (in fact, it would be better to speak of practices of liberation) because the various kinds of human liberation and, for that matter, even social liberation alone, involve the convergence of diverse activities on diverse levels. These levels of the Christian practice of liberation are mutually complementary and have a certain continuity among themselves, while maintaining their own autonomy and identity. Thus, the practice of political, social education and pastoral action, all of which have their own autonomy, are nevertheless united by a Christian — liberating — concern that interrelates them. In these cases, the church's spiritual tradition provides us with neither analyses, nor methods, nor concrete objectives. What it does offer us is a mystique (deep motivation) and an ethical attitude regarding interior liberation and a new method of relating to others in society.

The practice of interior liberation, which is a distinctive trait of Christian spirituality, is just as important as pastoral or political practices. There is no need to recall here that the Christian idea of liberation holds that, without human beings who are free, converted from the worship of their idols and made capable of fraternity, solidarity and justice, the processes of social liberation would stand in jeopardy.

In this sense, the Christian mystique is essentially liberating; it liberates us so that we in turn may liberate others. It reminds us that human oppressions, and the forms of injustice and servitude that human beings impose on other human beings cannot be eliminated by purely sociopolitical, economic, educational or psychological activities. It reminds us that in the message of the Bible, inner slavery and outer servitude are deeply linked. The vocation of the great mystics is to remind us of these elementary Christian truths, and above all, to inspire us by their own life-witness, so that each individual and each community may begin to journey along the path of inward liberation in order to be able to liberate others.

St. Ignatius of Loyola was an expert in this endeavor. The great project of his Christian life and that of the Society he founded was to uplift the world and liberate people from the miseries of the spirit and from all human misery, and this, in his view, was what constituted the service of the kingdom of Christ. But he was also keenly aware that this service of the kingdom implied the interior liberation of the liberators. His *Spiritual Exercises* are an itinerary of interior liberation through the imitation of Christ, in order to be able to work more effectively for his kingdom.

Liberation from Fetishes

Social analysts speak of the fetishes of society — the profit motive, production or consumption, money and power — as sources of servitude and injustice. In these analyses, they are not far from the notions of Christian spirituality, with its demands for conversion from the worship of the fetishes (the idols of society, in this case) which enslave the human heart. It is true, of course, that today's social sciences and ideologies propose to remedy this situation, not by espousing a process of Christian conversion, but only through the application of certain economic and sociopolitical measures. And herein lies the insufficiency of their proposals for human liberation. But herein, too, lies the reason for the importance of Christian mysticism in the struggle for justice, since it proposes an itinerary of inner liberation from idols and fetishes which no form of merely social practice can replace.

In this setting, the spiritual message of St. Teresa takes on a special significance. For one thing, she was keenly aware of the idols and fetishes (although she did not use these words) that enslaved the people of her time, including churchmen: wealth, power and honors. These idols were to be found in all degrees of idolatry ranging from blatant sins down to the subtle servitudes that she observed in her convents, and she saw that in every case they led to blindness of heart. Teresa was a past master at recognizing these blindnesses as a form of slavery of the conscience which prevented it from discerning where its true good and freedom lay:

> Some people have all they need and a good sum of money shut up in their safe as well. Because they avoid serious sins, they think they have done their duty. They enjoy their riches and give an occasional alms, yet never consider that their property is not their own, but that God has entrusted it to them to share with the poor. . . . We have no concern with this except to ask God to enlighten such people . . . and to thank Him for making us poor, which we should hold as a special favor on His part (*Conceptions of the Love of God*, Ch. II, par. 8).

This explains why Teresa was so demanding about poverty in all its dimensions, whether in matters of lifestyle or in detachment from honors and prestige. For her, poverty prepares us for light and liberty. Her writings abound in treatments of this theme, which is so close to our own experience: austerity and poverty of life as a component of solidarity with the needy and with their evangelization, as well as the need for a union of internal and external poverty so as to avoid the illusions and pharisaisms that can accompany our solidarity with the poor. Above all, she touches upon one quite current evangelical concern: the witness-value of the religious life (and indeed, of any form of Christian

life), as a counter-cultural sign of a way of living and valu-
ing things in opposition to the fetishes (honors, power and
money) of society and culture.

> What have I to do with kings and lords, if I do not
> seek their wealth? or with pleasing them, if by do-
> ing so I should be ever so little displeasing to God?
> And what are their honors to me, when I know that
> a poor person who is truly poor is as honorable as
> they? . . . Do you think, my daughters, that it re-
> quires but little virtue to deal with the world and
> live in the world, . . . and yet to live interiorly a
> stranger to the world, and enemy to the world? (*The
> Way of Perfection*, Ch. II, par. 5; Ch. III, par. 3).

Teresa's witness is particularly interesting in that her concept of the religious life includes a new form of relationship,
not only among the sisters themselves, but also between the
sister and the "outside world," based only on the criteria of
the gospel and not on the cultural prejudices of her age. With
the power and freedom that come from the Spirit, Teresa
had to overcome in herself, in relation to civil society, and
even in the church those prejudices against women which
were prevalent even in the domain of spirituality. In this domain it was taken for granted that women should be content
with vocal and external devotions and should not venture forth
along the roads of mysticism. By her own witness St. Teresa
contributed to the task of liberating spirituality from this
cultural and religious prejuduce for future generations. She
is one of the main witnesses of a stage in women's liberation.

> Now I turn to those who wish to follow this road,
> that is, until they attain a drink of this water of life
> . . . . It is important and even essential to take a firm
> resolve not to stop before we reach the font . . .
> come what may, happen what may . . . murmur who
> will. . . . As frequently happens the world will tire

itself repeating . . . "It is not for women, who are given to illusions"; "better that they should sew"; "they have no need of these refinements"; "the Paternoster and Ave Maria are enough for them" (*The Way of Perfection*, Ch. XXI, par 2).

Teresa also overcame social prejudices with regard to honors and distinctions. The theme of honor was very important in 16th-century Spanish society. As in all societies before and after it, there were dishonorable and discriminatory situations and circumstances, among which (and to our point here) there was the circumstance of Jewish ancestry. Today it seems to be a well-established fact that, in the paternal line, Teresa was descended from Jewish-Christian ancestors—which, by the way, was true of many families, even among the Spanish nobility. This point should not be overestimated in the experience of Teresa, but still she undoubtedly had to overcome this "fine point of honor" and lineage through the warmth of her friendship with Jesus.

And what are their [i.e., the powerful of this world] honors to me? (*The Way of Perfection*, Ch II, par. 5).

Are we striving after union with God, and . . . to follow the counsels of Christ, who was loaded with reproaches . . . and at the same time want to keep our honor and credit intact? . . . And in getting rid of that wretched honor, I learned how to do what I regarded as an honor, for everyone regards what he likes as honorable (*Life*, Ch. XXXI, par. 22 and 23).

Then he (Jesus) showed Himself to me . . very deeply within me, and told me: "From this day forward, you shall be my spouse . . . Now my honor is yours, and yours is mine" (*Relations* [or *Accounts of Conscience*], Avila, November 18, 1572).

The repeated occurrence in Teresa's writings of the theme of true and false honor, and the need for poverty in the face of worldly honors and distinctions is completely consistent with her particular experience of liberation from the fetishes of her society.

All of this has great relevance for us in connection with our own faith-mission. Evangelizing our own societies and cultures and working for the cause of justice requires that we, too, should introduce a new criterion and a new and evangelical form of social, egalitarian and fraternal form of social relationships, leaving behind all prejudices toward women and toward false honors and distinctions based on social class, race, prestige, or even religion.

St. Teresa undertook the reform of Carmel precisely in order to make the religious life a sign of liberation from all the idols of her time, as a counterculture and a counter-current to the spirit of the world. For her, the road that leads to this liberation is a true martyrdom—which, in the language of the mystics, means a daily dying to the idols of the body and the spirit. In the Teresian tradition, this daily death is the outcome of a constant practice of charity and fraternity.

> And do you not know, sisters, that the life of a good religious, who wishes to be among the closest friends of God, is one long martyrdom? (*The Way of Perfection*, Ch. XII, par. 2).

For Teresa, this death to idols through love would in turn create fraternity (solidarity). In this, too, she throws light on our own experience, in which we conceive liberation as related to fraternity and solidarity, and as a way toward communion and sharing. This is also the place where the spirit of martyrdom fits into the picture of Christian liberation. But Teresa does not stop at a "spiritualization" of martyrdom; her daily dying to whatever is not the freedom of love, is the best preparation to merit the grace of "real" martyrdom (giving one's life out of great love for the kingdom) which she ardently longed for.

> It seems certain to me that in order to free one alone from such appalling torments I would suffer many deaths very willingly (*Life*, Ch. XXXII, par. 6).

As a spirituality of martyrdom, the message of St. Teresa has a special importance for our generation. It reminds us that authentic Christian martyrdom is a grace that is won through daily abnegation and love and cannot be prefabricated or improvised. It reminds us that all forms of martyrdom and persecution are incompatible with the triumphalism and "Christian glory" that sometimes attend them, and which are usually just one more subtle foxhole in which self-love and blindness of heart take refuge.

"Liberating God"

Today the spiritual-theological issue of liberation and justice also entails the "God-problem": What kind of God do we have? What kind of God do we adore and follow? Is our God the authentic God of Christianity, the God of the Bible, the God who is the Father of Jesus Christ, or is he, rather, the God whom we have consciously or unconsciously deformed and manipulated in order to accommodate him to our interests, ideology or culture?

This is a problem for our spirituality and a matter for our conversion: We must abandon this impure idea of God, and be converted to the one, true God, a God who cannot be manipulated, who is a God of mercy, justice and fraternity, a God who has a predilection for the poor. Only if we believe in and follow *this* God, will our Christian spirituality develop its dimensions of commitment to and with the poor, to and with justice.

To liberate God from the deformations we have introduced
into the notion of God is a spiritual problem; to allow this
God to act in us and communicate his qualities to us is a
spiritual problem. To unite ourselves to this God and not to
an idol is also a spiritual problem—and all these cases affect
our attitude toward others and toward justice. The heart of
God will lead us to the heart of the poor. We are called to
union with the God who is inseparable from justice and
mercy—and this is precisely what consitutes the mystical
journey.

St. John of the Cross is the spiritual theologian who has
most extensively and profoundly exposed the deformations
which we usually introduce into our relationship with God,
as well as the ways to overcome them in order to become
united with the authentic Christian God. St. John of the Cross
"liberates God": He teaches us to let God be God, and to
let God change us according to his Spirit.

> A man, then, is decidedly hindered from the attain-
> ment of this high state of union with God when he
> is attached to any understanding, feeling, imagining,
> opinion, desire, or way of his own, or to any other
> of his works or affairs, and knows not how to de-
> tach and denude himself of these impediments. . . .
> Entering on the road [of union] means leaving one's
> own road, and [this] implies entry into what has no
> mode, that is, God (*Ascent*, Book II, Ch. 4, Nos.
> 4 and 5).

> The preparation for this union, as we said, is not an
> understanding by the soul, nor the taste, feeling, or
> imagining of God or any other object, but purity and
> love, which is the stripping off and perfect renun-
> ciation of all these experiences for God alone. . . .
> For to love is to labor to divest and deprive oneself
> for God of all that is not God. When this is done

the soul will be illumined by and transformed in God
(*Ascent*, Book II, Ch. 5, Nos. 8 and 7).

Since there can be no Christian liberation without the
"liberation of God," this message of St. John of the Cross
is a contribution of primary importance.

John's *Dark Night* is the itinerary that helps us find God
without deforming him. *The Spiritual Canticle* and *The Living Flame of Love* are the transcript of an experience of union
with God liberated from our servitudes, who transmits to us
his mode of being and of acting. In John's spiritual synthesis,
we liberate God from imperfect ways of being united to him
and imitating him through the purification of faith (the faculty
which unites us with God as he is), and through the purification of love (from its lies and selfishness). These purifications are accomplished through liberating deaths and crosses:

> O, who can explain the extent of the denial our Lord
> wishes of us! This negation must be similar to a com-
> plete temporal, natural and spiritual death. . . . Our
> Savior referred to this when He declared: *He who
> wishes to save his life shall lose it, and he who loses
> his soul for my sake, the same shall gain it.* The latter
> affirmation signifies: He who renounces for Christ
> all that his will can desire and enjoy . . . which our
> Lord in St. John terms hating one's own life [Jn
> 22:25]—the same will gain it (*Ascent*, Book II, Ch.
> 7, No. 6).

He calls these purifications whereby we allow God to be God
for us *las noches*, the night of the senses and the night of
the spirit which liberate faith for a true encounter with God.
Only this noctural death to false experiences of God can unite
us to the authentic God of Jesus, of the poor, and of universal fraternity. All other means of mediating and of imaging
God bear the stamp of our imperfections and manipulations
and are incompatible with the God of radical faith and love.

For in place of this real God, they substitute a God drawn from our imagination, according to the measure of our own cravings. That is why, among the three preliminary tasks for the ascent of Mount Carmel, John begins as follows: "First, he must cast out the strange gods, all alien affections and attachments (*Ascent*, Book I, Ch. 5, No. 7).

One of the major difficulties in reading and comprehending St. John of the Cross stems from his use of symbolic and poetic language. One key concept that can open his teaching to a contemporary reading is the notion of the liberation of God or our own inner liberation. This can bring us to a better understanding of his symbols of nights or of nothingnesses. The same can be said of his symbols of solitude, by which John does not mean isolation or loneliness, but rather, a "resonant solitude" filled with God and leading to union with him. In this connection, too, St. John of the Cross throws light on the themes of retreat and the desert which have regained their full importance in modern spirituality. The desert is a form of deep liberation; it compels us to face the truth about all realities and about ourselves, stripped of the illusions and lies that dwell in us and in society, and this truth sets us free. The resonant solitude of which he speaks implies at once the silence of words that oppress and lie, and the sound of God's word that brings liberation.

The values of solitude and a liberating desert experience, both of which are so strongly emphasized in Carmelite mysticism, are also an important part of the search for spirituality in the contemporary world, which is oppressed by the deceptions of the mass media, by the relentless pace of too much activity, by the evasive pursuit of too much amusement, and by a seeming incapacity to find the solitude it needs for renewal and fulfillment.

Thus, all of the symbols used by St. John of the Cross (night, nothingness, mountain, flame, solitude, desert, etc.)

as well as his many apt comparisons (the slender thread that
binds the bird, the wood in the fire, the light and the ray
of darkness, the soiled windowpane, and others are symbols
of the progressive purification of our relationship with God,
wherein God is liberated from our deformations and ideolo-
gizing and is revealed as the God for others and for the life
of the world.

CONCLUSION

The presence—latent or explicit—of the great Spanish mystics can still be felt in the spiritual tradition that has continued to develop from the 16th century to our day. This presence is manifest in the survival of their values (although some have been weakened by changing times and a de-Christianized environment): their sense of God and of the religious meaning of life; their firm belief in our capacity for prayer and for conformity with God's will; their realism and wisdom in facing the heights, depths and plateaus of the human condition; their esteem for emotion and affection in religious life and language; their devotion to the suffering humanity of Christ; their deep appreciation of the church, not only as teacher, but as the "place" of Christian life.

The message of the mystics is strikingly valid for the spiritual search that is emerging today out of the Christian and pastoral experience of our communities. If this search is to be authentic and lasting, it must be rooted both in our own experience and in the spiritual tradition of the church—of which the Spanish mystics are the finest expression. Their teaching should be called upon to provide our faith with a fundamental inspiration and firm roots in the true experience of God. These classics of spirituality can be read with immense value by every Christian generation, including our own, provided they are set in proper perspective and given an adequate re-reading.

We cannot go on nourishing our spirituality on secondhand materials. We need to let Ignatius, Teresa and John speak to us directly. Even the most summary survey of the contemporary religious scene should bring this lesson home to us. If today the *Spiritual Exercises* of St. Ignatius are still being preached; if during the fourth centennial of St. Teresa her writings have been featured in magazine articles and in seminars and conferences for their relevance to our Christian situation; and if St. John of the Cross is still the central figure for university faculties and serious studies on contemporary spirituality, it should be clear to us that it is because the richness of their spirit is not only a legacy of the past, but also a priceless possession of the present and a guarantee of our future.